THE BARRINGTON GUIDE TO PROPERTY MANAGEMENT ACCOUNTING

PHILLIP GAVIN BARRINGTON

THE BARRINGTON GUIDE TO PROPERTY MANAGEMENT ACCOUNTING

Dedicated to Jesse for your love and support

Copyright © 2023 by PHILLIP GAVIN BARRINGTON
All rights reserved. No part of this book may be reproduced in any manner whatsoever without written permission except in the case of brief quotations embodied in critical articles and reviews.
Second Printing, 2025

FOREWORD

To property owners reading this book: *You can do this!* If you recently acquired your first property, you'll find this book invaluable to understanding how to set up your accounting books. Even if this is your 15th property, this book will still be very useful, because I'll show you some tips and tricks you might not have known before. I grew up in a household where my parents owned and managed multiple million-dollar apartment buildings all by themselves. They fixed what needed fixing, they signed up new tenants when needed, and they called and relied on professionals when needed.

To property managers reading this book: *You can do this!* If this is your first job in property management, this book will help you immensely. Even if you are an experienced property manager, you will find valuable information that will further assist with your management.

When I think back to the early days of my accounting career, I realize I didn't choose real estate management accounting – it chose me. I was taking accounting classes while doing bookkeeping for a friend's apartment rental property, as my parents had sold off the bulk of their real estate holdings. After school finished, I turned those skills into a hybrid property manager/bookkeeper role.

I sent out tenant invoices, reconciled bank accounts, managed buildouts, performed lease reviews, made tenant collection calls, reported tenant-in-common financials to multiple owners and performed Common Area Maintenance reconciliations for over 100+

tenants (which we will later talk about in detail). These tenants were of varying types, big box stores, mom and pop shops, restaurant startups, banks, jewelers, fast food restaurants, a brewery, hair salons, nail salons, tax preparation offices, among many others.

Managing all these tenants was a full-time job on its own and adding the accounting to the mix made it a sink or swim situation. I dove in with both feet and relished the opportunities to learn and grow in a burgeoning field. Five years later, when I moved across the country for new opportunities, I was ready to take the skills I attained and apply them to a whole new market.

To those property management accountants and bookkeepers reading this book: *You can do this!* If you just started working in property management accounting, this book will be a great help. Or if you are a seasoned veteran, you will find the information presented useful, and can use this book as a reference.

Let's go back to my first day at the property management company. I had a week with the prior occupant of my position to learn as much as I could. I still remember the owners, who didn't involve themselves with the accounting end, asked if I knew the difference between a statement and an invoice. The prior accountant said, "Well if he doesn't, he should walk out the door right now." We all laughed, and I respected that she was not going to baby me, even as she was entering her retirement within a week's time. At that time, my accounting education was much more general, and not geared to any one specialty. Having a general accounting knowledge can be both helpful and a hindrance, depending on what kind of accountant you want to be. It was extremely helpful in this case, because it allowed me to take in all the specific nuances of Property Management accounting without bias.

As accountants, I am part of a group where we can apply the accounting principles and best practices we learned in school to almost any field. However, to know the intricacies of accounting requires experience, as it does in most fields. So, while many can figure out how to use popular accounting software to create an invoice and make a statement, the underlying rules of accounting are not usually known unless taught.

After a week with the prior accountant (that was mostly filled with going away lunches and happy hour trips) I was left that next Monday, by myself, feeling a bit overwhelmed. I wanted to know as much information about property management accounting as I could, so I could do the best job possible. I went to the local bookstore, because there has to be a plethora of beginning real estate accounting books, right? There were some, with odd titles, but nothing clearly for what I needed. I still ordered a few, figuring I could piece together a beginner's guide.

Many were about property purchasing, but alarmingly few about accounting *after* purchasing. Other accounting books were very high-level (with a high *dry*-level of writing) and were well above what I needed for my position at the time. I felt a little like Goldilocks, where *just right* was unattainable. Next, I went to the internet. I searched many websites, and while general accounting information is plentiful, there was no site that was specific enough for what I needed. No one had written a book, or developed a website, on how to do property management accounting. I was shocked, as property management firms are very prevalent in most markets, and property owners are everywhere.

Slowly I learned on my own, with help from the company's tax CPA, and by examining and learning how property management and ownership worked. Combining this hands-on learning with knowledge of the underlying accounting, I grew in confidence and experience. But I could have skipped a lot of aggravation if someone would have provided some basic accounting specific to property management. This need for better understanding property management accounting was even more crucial at my next position – an accountant at a large CPA firm.

At the firm I handled accounting for all types of businesses – from doctor's offices, to betting companies to copyright holding companies

– and all in between. But my specialty was property management accounting. I had all kinds of clients in the real estate market: commercial, residential, industrial, mixed use, and governmental properties. I ended up doing everything: sending out monthly statements and invoices, preparing financial statements, creating rent rolls, managing accounts payable and accounts receivable for all different types of owners and ownership groups, reconciling Common Area Maintenance (CAM), managing shared ownership CAM, booking depreciation and amortization, and making complex budgeting and forecasting models – among many other things.

I've always said, the reason you hire an accountant is because we know the underlying reasoning behind all the transactions a business makes. Basing decisions on that understanding allows a company and its owners to analyze and focus on the right financial markers to better improve their business.

After a few years at the CPA firm, I was approached by a private equity firm specializing in real estate holdings. I was given control of all accounting while also cross-training new property managers on the basics of real estate accounting. They all had a varying degree of understanding of the underlying accounting to what they were doing. Most understood invoicing and statements, a few had taken some accounting classes in college, and the best knew of Common Area Maintenance Reconciliations (CAM Recs for short). So, I created a two-page basic summary on what they needed to know right away. Then, over time we would go over the more complex parts as required. And that's where this book started.

As a property owner (and I have worked with many) it's really important to understand exactly how you make money (its deeper than just rent collection), how to continue to make money, and how to grow and turn your property into multiple properties, if you want. As a property manager, in order to make money for your clients, you will need to understand the accounting that goes into being a successful property manager. As you read on, make notes, highlight passages, dog ear pages, and use this book as a reference tool, that's why I wrote it.

This introduction has given a taste of my writing style, which is how I also work. I try to be precise and to the point, while also understandable – a trait I used in management. I have trained many employees, and I believe in empowerment as more than just a catch phrase. If a job is clearly explained, proper tools provided and the expectations spelled out, then an employee has the freedom to bring their personal style to perform the work.

I will provide the knowledge I have gained through experience to make property management easier for you, whether you are an owner, a manager or new bookkeeper like I once was. I will do this in a concise and understandable way to provide you the keys to a successfully run property. You will have the tools. The rest is up to you. Good luck!

Phillip Gavin Barrington

Disclaimer: The information provided in this book is for educational purposes only, to assist in property management. It is not intended to be a source of financial or legal advice. Making adjustments to a financial strategy or plan should only be undertaken after consulting with a professional. The publisher and the author make no guarantee of financial results or success obtained by using this book, but I certainly think it will help!

CONTENTS

Dedication   iv
Foreword   vii

PART I   1
1 Accounting History   2
2 Debits and Credits   4
3 The General Ledger and Journal Entries   7
4 Types of Accounts   10
5 Financial Statements   13
6 The Profit and Loss Statement   15
7 The Balance Sheet   18
8 Chart of Accounts   21
9 Bank Reconciliations   27

PART II   31
10 Property Types   32
11 Residential Properties   33
12 Commercial and Industrial Properties   36
13 Leases   39
14 Lease Types: All-in versus Triple-Net   41

15	Invoicing and Statements	45
16	Common Area Maintenance (CAM) and HOA Dues	50
17	Determining Correct amounts for Triple Net Charges	53
18	Triple Net Reconciliations	56
19	CAM Recording Correctly to Make Reconciliations	60
20	Rent Rolls	63
PART III		66
21	Hire a Property Management Co or Manage Yourself	67
22	Managing it Yourself	69
23	Hiring a Property Management Company	71
24	Leasing Agents, Brokers, and Real Estate Lawyers	76
25	Hiring Contractors and Choosing Vendors	79
26	Choosing and working with a CPA	82
27	Other Consultants	86
28	1099s	87
PART IV		90
29	Cash Basis and Accrual Basis Accounting	91
30	Cash Basis Accounting	92
31	Accrual Basis Accounting	95
32	Cash or Accrual Accounting: Which is Right for You	97
33	Accounts Payable, Accounts Receivable and Bad Debt	100
34	Fixed Assets: To Capitalize or Not to Capitalize	106
35	Tenant Improvements, Buildouts, and Whiteboxing	110
36	Depreciation and Amortization for Accounting	114

37	Depreciation and Accumulated Depreciation	116
38	Amortization for Property Management	119
39	How to Record a Purchase Closing Statement	123
40	Gain or Loss on Building Sale	127
PART V		130
41	Section 1: First Quarter, Year One	131
42	Section 2: Two Years Later	147

ACKNOWLEDGEMENT	156
About the Author	157
Books by this Author	158

PART I

Introduction to Basic Accounting (with examples for Property Management)

We begin with:

- A brief history of accounting
- Definitions of common accounting terms
- An explanation of important financial statements
- A review of bank reconciliations

This information will provide you with a solid accounting foundation.

CHAPTER 1

Accounting History

Accounting has been around since humans began trading goods and services, soon after we moved from hunter-gathers to farmers. Some ancient civilizations kept meticulous accounting records on stone tablets that have survived to this day. These records reveal that the more things change, the more they stay the same.

Early accounting was more primitive, but as accounts grew larger, and trade became more extensive and global, people began looking for more efficient ways to account for transactions. It eventually led to what is now known as double-entry bookkeeping.

In 13th Century Renaissance Italy, double-entry bookkeeping was created by a monk named Luca Pacioli and we still use this method today. Double-entry bookkeeping means that for any transaction that occurs in a business that either involves money or will involve money there is a record of the transaction in at least two accounts (which we will expand more upon shortly). Most importantly, Pacioli established the basic accounting equation, which is:

Assets = Liabilities + Equity

This is easily interpreted as: Everything you own is equal to everything you owe *plus* your equity (ownership) in the company. Let us look at an example.

Example 1.1:

You purchased a property worth $10 million. You took out a loan of $9 million and paid $1 million of your own money to purchase the property. The accounting equation specific to this transaction is:

Property	=	Outstanding Loan	+ Investment
$10 million Property	=	$9M Loan	+ $1M Investment
Asset	=	Liability	+ Equity

The next step is recording the transaction. Every accounting transaction is recorded in the General Journal. The General Journal is the record of all accounting transactions that occur for a business. This is detailed on a report called the General Ledger which we will delve into further in a later chapter. Next, we will discuss how the transaction is recorded in the General Ledger using Debits and Credits.

CHAPTER 2

Debits and Credits

Your first experience with debits and credits is usually with your personal bank statement. On the bank statement you see debits and credits. Whenever you deposit money into your account it is called a **credit** and a payment is referred to as a **debit**. (This is correct but not in the way many of us are used to). Debiting (or crediting) an account means that you either increased (or decreased) that account, depending on the account type. For every debit amount there must be an equal credit amount.

The most important distinction here is to *never* think of debits and credits in terms of "positives" and "negatives." Rather think of them as either increasing or decreasing their account balance. How that works is based on the type of account it is. Let us look at an example.

Example 2.1:

You pay an electrician $1,500 to replace an electric service panel at one of your properties. This is an **Expense** Transaction. The journal entry to record this transaction is:

Debit: Electrical Repairs Expense for $1,500 (your expense increases)
Credit: Bank Account for $1,500 (your bank account decreases)

Example 2.2: Here is an example of an **Income** transaction:

Your tenant pays you $2,000 for the monthly rent. The journal entry to record this transaction is:

Debit: Bank Account for $2,000 (your bank account increases)
Credit: Rental Income for $2,000 (your income increases)

"Wait wait!" you say, "When I take money in, I *debit* my bank account and when I paid that electrician isn't that a *credit*? That's not right, is it? Because when I look at my bank statement when money comes in it's a credit on my account, not a debit. What gives?"

Here is the important distinction: these transactions are *from the bank's perspective*, not yours (or your company). So, when you deposit money into your bank account you say, "the bank credited my account" and that is true, because from the *bank's perspective* the person who paid you took money from their account (credit) and added it to yours (debit). However, on *your books*, the transaction increased your cash, which is a debit. Confusing, right?

The best way to combat this conundrum is to always think of the bank as *backwards*. Once you do that and *know* that every time money comes into your bank account it is a debit, you will easily solve what I call the bank conundrum.

Now let's stop and take a breath (a *deep* breath, breathe in through your nose, hold it, and out through your mouth) and think about all you have just read about debits and credits. Let me take a guess – you just skimmed after you read the words debit and credit, right? That is perfectly fine, there is nothing wrong about being confused about debits and credits and having complete knowledge of them is not required to run a successful business. As we go along, we will look at more of the reasoning behind debits and credits, so there will be more opportunities to explore this concept. And really – you do not need to be an expert on debits and credits. But the knowledge of how they work is important when you are reviewing your financials and talking with your bookkeeper and/or accountant.

If you *really* want to understand the basics of debits and credits and accounting in general, I highly recommend taking an Introduction to Accounting course at your local community college. It is usually inexpensive and I suspect you'll get a teacher who really cares about teaching you accounting. Also, you can focus on what you want to learn from the class since you do not need it for graduation purposes.

Alternatively, you can hire a bookkeeper (or accountant depending on the size of your business) and then quiz them on their knowledge of debits and credits. If they can demonstrate an understanding of what you've read thus far, you have found an accountant that has a solid knowledge base in accounting.

Just to reiterate, as this is the most important piece of information to know about accounting: Any transaction that occurs is always recorded using a minimum of two accounts, using at least one debit and at least one credit. These transactions are recorded on the General Ledger, which we will look at in the next chapter.

CHAPTER 3

The General Ledger and Journal Entries

The General Ledger, or GL for short, is are records of all the transactions (debits and credits) that occur over a period of time. Your GL is often referred to as your "Books." At the base level, these transactions are all recorded through **Journal Entries**. Let us look at an example.

Example 3.1:

On January 2nd, you pay an electrician $1,500 to replace an electric service panel at one of your properties, which is same as Example 2.1 from the previous chapter. Here is the Journal Entry required to record the transaction:

Debit: Electrical Repairs Expense   *$1,500*
Credit: Bank Account   *$1,500*

The General Ledger is a report that your accountant will often request to prepare your business tax return. The time period is usually January 1st through December 31st, which is the typical Fiscal Year of most companies and of personal income tax returns. However, the General Ledger report can be for any time period.

You may also hear the term "General Journal" which is often used interchangeably with General Ledger. There is actually a difference between the two, but for our purposes, we'll focus on the more important General Ledger. The following information is usually found on a General Ledger report:

- Date
- Account Name and Number (if used)
- Check Number
- Payee or Payor
- Memo/Description of the transaction
- Whether the amount is a debit or credit
- A running total

Let us look at a further example.

Example 3.2:

Here is the General Ledger for the period, which in this case is January to December. You can see the Account Name, Date of the transaction, the Check number, the Vendor or Payee, the Memo/Description which describes what the payment is for, and the Debit and Credit columns. Since you paid cash for the work performed, your cash account is reduced by $1,500. The Electrical Repairs Expense is increased by the same $1,500.

Your Property Company
General Ledger
For the Period of January - December 20XX

Account	Date	Check #	Vendor	Memo/Description	Debit	Credit	Total
Cash/Bank							
	1/2/XX	1001	Best Electric	Service Panel Replacement		1,500	-1,500
Total Cash/Bank							-1,500
Electrical Repairs Expense							
	1/2/XX	1001	Best Electric	Service Panel Replacement	1,500		1,500
Total Electrical Repairs Expense							1,500

As an owner, you may not use the General Ledger as often as the Profit and Loss Statement or Balance Sheet, however if detail on a transaction is needed, the General Ledger is where to look. The General Ledger is organized by account type. Next, we will look at the five different types of accounts.

CHAPTER 4

Types of Accounts

There are five categories of accounts:

- Assets
- Liabilities
- Equity/Capital
- Income
- Expenses

In the General Ledger the accounts appear in this order. These five can have many subcategories but any type of account you can think of fits into one of these five. Let us look at some examples of each type of account:

Assets: bank accounts, accounts receivable and other money that is owed to you, tangible assets such as land, buildings, vehicles, etc.; as well as intangible assets such as trademarks and copyrights, prepaid expenses, etc.

Liabilities: accounts payable, outstanding loans or notes, security deposits received, etc.

Equity/Capital: equity invested in the entity, retained earnings (from previous years Net Income), distributions/draws to owners, etc.

Income: revenue from sources such as rent, service income, sales, late fees, etc.

Expenses: utilities, office supplies, rent, management fees, repairs and maintenance, landscaping, janitorial, etc. For most businesses, the Expenses category will have the greatest number of accounts.

The type of account will tell you whether it has a normal debit balance or credit balance. So when a transaction occurs, it will normally increase or decrease based on its normal debit or credit balance. The Assets and Expenses categories have normal debit balances, while Liabilities, Equity/Capital, and Income categories have normal credit balances.

Any accounting class will teach you the easiest way to understand accounts and their appropriate debit and credit balance is to use T-Accounts (because they look like a T ... isn't that creative?). For T-accounts, debits are on the left-hand side, and credits are the right-hand side. Let's record a couple transactions using T-Accounts. We will use the same examples from the previous chapter.

Example 4.1:

You pay an electrician $1,500 to replace an electric service panel at one of your properties. As we noted in the prior chapter, the transaction debits the Electrical Repairs Expense account and credits the Bank Account. See below for how it looks using T-Accounts:

Electrical Repairs Expense		Bank Account	
Debit	Credit	Debit	Credit
1,500			1,500

Example 4.2:

Next, your tenant pays you $2,000 for the monthly rent. In Example 2.2, we saw that this transaction was recorded as a credit to Income for $2,000 and a debit to the Bank Account for $2,000. See below for how it looks using T-Accounts:

Rental Income		Bank Account	
Debit	Credit	Debit	Credit
	2,000	2,000	1,500

The bank account balance after both transactions increased by $500, which is the deposit of $2,000 less the expense of $1,500.

$500 (Debit Balance) = $2,000 (Debit Increase) - $1,500 (Credit Decrease)

Using and understanding T-Accounts is not necessary to successful property ownership and management, but it should still be mentioned for comprehensiveness. It can also help you understand debits and credits by being able to track them in a basic way. Next, we will move on to a much more important topic, Financial Statements.

CHAPTER 5

Financial Statements

Financial Statements are summaries of the transactions that occur over a given period or as of a certain date. They can quickly tell an owner how much money they have made (or lost) as well as other pertinent information about their business. Financial Statements are key to reviewing, maintaining, and later, growing your business.

There are many different financial statements that can provide a multitude of useful data to assess your property and business. You will hear the following statements mentioned most often, and should review these reports on a regular basis:

- Balance Sheet
- Profit and Loss Statement
- Accounts Payable Report
- Accounts Receivable Report (also known as the Tenant Receivables Report)
- Rent Roll (updated monthly)
- General Ledger
- Bank Reconciliation Report

We have already looked at the General Ledger, and we'll review the other types of statements in subsequent chapters. Beginning property owners and managers should start with the two main financial statements used in property management accounting: The Balance Sheet and the Profit and Loss Statement. These two statements will also be used by owners (as well as by your CPA to prepare your taxes) in making sound financial decisions about their properties.

CHAPTER 6

The Profit and Loss Statement

The Profit and Loss Statement (often shortened to the P&L) is also known as the Income Statement. This statement shows your income from your property and the expenses associated with it for a period of time.

Profit and Loss Statements can contain multiple subtotals, and in the example you see three: Gross Income, Total Expenses and Net Income. Gross Income is simple; it is your Income before your expenses. Total Expenses are the total of all the expenses incurred in the period of reporting. Finally, Net Income is your Gross Income less your Total Expenses. This could also be considered the Profit (or Loss) of your property. Let us look at a sample Profit and Loss Statement.

Example 6.1:

Company XYZ
Profit and Loss Statement
For the Period of January to December 20XX

Rental Income	$ 210,000	
Other Income	1,050	
Gross Income		211,050
Landscaping	4,400	
Trash	3,600	
Electric	4,800	
Water	1,800	
Office Supplies	1,900	
Property Taxes Paid	22,000	
Insurance	6,000	
Repairs and Maintenance	25,000	
Legal Fees	3,000	
Settlement Fees	5,000	
Interest Expense	18,000	
Total Expenses		95,500
Net Income		$ 115,550

The Profit and Loss Statement can be run for any time period – the entire year, a quarter, a month, and even one day. In our above example, the period is for an entire year. It can be very beneficial to look at the Profit and Loss Statement by month and by quarter, as that can show trends and consistency (or lack thereof) in collections and expenses. Also, for entities that have been in business more than one year, comparing two (or more) years can also provide data that management/ownership can use to assess the entity.

One common assessment is profitability. Businesses use their Profit and Loss Statements to figure out whether expenses are too high, and if so, how to lower them. Or they may assess why rents are lower compared to the previous year. We will look at a Comparative Profit and Loss Statement in a later chapter. The Profit and Loss Statement can also assist in budgeting as well as forecasting, which are things that a growing property owner will want to look at to prepare for the future.

The Profit and Loss Statement connects to the Balance Sheet, as the Net Income (or Loss) will be found in the Equity Section on the Balance Sheet, as we will see in the next chapter.

CHAPTER 7

The Balance Sheet

The Balance Sheet shows what the company owns (Assets), what it owes (Liabilities), and Owner Investment (Equity) of an entity at a certain *point* in time. That distinction is important and that differentiates it from the Profit and Loss Statement, which covers a *period* of time. The Balance Sheet is run as of a certain date – usually the end of a period – whether that is the end of a month, a quarter, or a year. But in reality, it can be run at any date. It is a report that shows the accounting equation, which we previously saw in Chapter One:

Assets = Liabilities + Equity

The Balance Sheet is important because it tells the reader what the status is of the entity as of a certain date. Does the entity have enough cash in the bank? That is found in the Asset section. How many assets does the entity have? How much debt is there? How much equity? The answers to these questions can be found on the Balance Sheet.

As mentioned above, the Net Income is also found on the Balance Sheet, so you can see how profitable the company is (at a point in time) without needing to look at the Profit and Loss Statement. This is because the Net Income (or Loss) is the property of ownership, and the Net Income is found in the Equity section of the Balance Sheet. Let us look at a sample Balance Sheet.

Example 7.1:

Company XYZ
Balance Sheet
For the Period Ended 12/31/XX

1000	Cash/Bank Account		166,550
1400	Building		800,000
1500	Land		200,000
1600	Loan Fees		50,000
1700	Leasing Commissions		2,000
Total Assets		$	1,218,550
2000	Loan		440,000
2200	Security Deposits		30,000
Total Liabilities			470,000
3000 Equity			633,000
Net Income			115,550
			748,550
Total Liabilities + Equity		$	1,218,550

As you can see, the total assets are equal to the total liabilities, plus equity. In this example, the entity has a Bank Account with $5,000, plus it owns a building booked at $100,000, and land booked at $50,000. Note that I said booked, instead of valued, or cost. The price that could be attained by selling, are not necessarily equal to the amounts booked on the Balance Sheet. Further detail on the booking of assets will be found in the chapter 39 "How to Record a Purchase Closing Statement."

In the Liabilities section there are two items: a loan of $120,000 and a Credit Card Payable of $1,000. In the equity section, there is the initial Owner Equity of $30,750 and Net Income of $3,250. Let us look at the Accounting Equation using these real numbers.

Example 7.2:

Assets = Liabilities + Equity

$155,000 = $121,000 + $34,000

Bank Account + Building + Land = Loan + Credit Card Payable + Owner Equity + Net Income

If a company has investors, their investment will be found in the Equity section of the Balance Sheet. If there is a single owner, the Equity section will be what the owner invested. Many may feel that the Balance Sheet is not nearly as important as the Profit and Loss Statement (because many owners want to see profits first, which is understandable). But keeping a correct balance sheet is necessary for sustained success – especially once ownership has occurred for a number of years. Tracking of changes and additions to assets, as well as liabilities, can show how a company has fared over time. Lastly, a Balance Sheet is also found on the Tax Return, and an up-to-date Balance Sheet will be needed by your CPA to prepare your tax return at the end of the fiscal year.

CHAPTER 8

Chart of Accounts

The Chart of Accounts is the list of accounts that will be used to record financial transactions in the General Ledger. Each specific account created will fall into one of the five categories that have been mentioned already but will be restated here: Assets, Liabilities, Capital, Income, and Expenses. It's crucial to set up the Chart of Accounts before you start recording transactions. Beware of inconsistencies in your Chart of Accounts, especially if multiple people are creating accounts. These inconsistencies can lead to confusion, duplicate accounts, and more time spent (and thus more money) when the accountant or CPA has to "clean it up" to prepare a tax return.

For instance, one owner I knew originally created a catch-all account called utilities, and then hired a bookkeeper to straighten out the Chart of Accounts, because she wanted more detail on her expenses. When the bookkeeper reviewed the monthly expenses, he had to separate the utilities (electric, gas, water, etc.) account into the specific accounts – which was time consuming. And if your CPA (who is more expensive) has to clean up messy accounting and make adjustments to prepare the tax return, your business will likely be charged extra for the work to prepare your General Ledger. It's better to set up the Chart of Accounts correctly before you start to save money and time.

Of course, new accounts will still have to be created as new expenses arise, but a good set up can lead to less confusion as the business grows.

Usually, the five categories of accounting receive their own beginning number designation for ease. Let us look at some header accounts.

Example 8.1:
Sample types of accounts with account numbers:
1000   Assets
2000   Liabilities
3000   Capital
4000   Income
6000   Expense

In accounting, the 5000 accounts are used for Cost of Goods Sold, typically. For property ownership there is nothing that is produced, so those numbers are skipped. You can number your accounts in any way you choose, but using the standard numbering keeps it simpler for your CPA, and what have we learned so far? That it keeps your bill from them lower.

You can then use sequential numbering for your different asset accounts, liability accounts, and so on. For example, let us say you have three bank accounts. The internal account number you may use for Account One is 1001, for Account Two is 1002, and for Account Three is 1003. You can use as many or as few digits as you wish but using four- or five-digit account numbers allow easy addition of new accounts as they arise, and is most standard.

Subcategories can also be used to summarize similar accounts for ease in reading your financial statements. For example, you may want to track all your utilities as one expense (if you own single family homes, for instance) or you may want to track them all individually. If so, there would be separate accounts for Electric, Gas, Telephone, Water, Sewer, etc. Here is an example as it could look on the Profit and Loss Statement.

Example 8.2:

Utilities	$500	Utilities	
		Electric	$150
		Water	$150
		Sewer	$25
		Gas	$125
		Telephone	$50
		Total Utilities	$500

The type of property you own or manage will help determine how detailed you want the Chart of Accounts to be. Here is a sample Chart of Accounts that could be used to start a new property company.

Example 8.3: (Account Number | Account Name)

1000	Cash on Hand
1001	Bank Account #1 - Income
1002	Bank Account #2 - Expenses
1003	Bank Account #3 - Savings
1200	Accounts Receivable
1400	Building
1450	Building Improvements
1500	Land
1550	Land Improvements
1600	Loan Fees

1700	Leasing Commissions
2000	Loan
2100	Accounts Payable
2200	Security Deposits
3000	Owner Equity
4000	Rental Income
4100	CAM Income
4200	Insurance Income
4300	Property Tax Income
4400	Late Fee Income
4500	Other Income
5000	Cost of Goods Sold
6000	Gas
6010	Electric
6020	Water
6030	Trash
6040	Sewer
6050	Other Utilities
6060	Telephone
6070	Security
6080	Fire Sprinklers

6090	Landscaping
6100	HVAC Repairs
6110	Property Taxes Paid
6120	Insurance
6130	Repairs and Maintenance
6140	Plumbing Repairs
6150	Painting
6160	Electrical Repairs
6170	Parking Lot Repairs
6180	Roof Repairs
6190	Internet
6200	Cleaning Fees
6210	Payroll
6200	Payroll Taxes
6210	Management Fees
6220	Office Expenses
6230	Miscellaneous Expenses
6240	Legal Fees
6250	Accounting Fees
6260	Consulting Fees
6270	Interest Expense

6280	Depreciation
6290	Amortization
6300	Capital Expenditures

If you purchase accounting software, they usually come pre-programed with a standard chart of accounts. You can then add or delete accounts as necessary to fit your business. Many can also be pre-programed to assign a specific account to a specific transaction. For example, when the electric company charges your account and the description reads "XYZ Electric" the software will automatically assign the Electric account designation, which saves time in the present and in the long run.

CHAPTER 9

Bank Reconciliations

Many of you may remember the term "balancing your checkbook" when personal bank checks were prevalent. The technical term in accounting is performing a Bank Reconciliation. A Bank Reconciliation is taking your ledger and comparing it to what the bank recorded as activity on your monthly bank statement.

The reconciling part is done by "matching" transactions that occurred on both your ledger and the bank statement. You then review transactions that were on the bank statement and not your ledger, and vice versa. You are reconciling the ending bank balance to the balance on your ledger as of the period end.

Bank Reconciliations (bank recs for short) may seem like a real pain to do and not all that important. For these reasons, some businesses avoid doing bank recs at all. I have met many property owners and managers that say, "I'll balance it at the end of the year. As long as my balance is positive, everything is ok." Others simply capitulate and say, "I'll just let my CPA handle it."

There's a huge danger to avoiding performing bank recs: *potential fraud*. If a check or outgoing wire is found on the bank statement but not on your ledger, it could be fraudulent and needs further investigation. Many banks are quite good at catching fraud, but I have seen some very sophisticated fraud. Almost always we were able detect the fraud by scrutinizing the bank rec (if not sooner).

I have seen all types of fraud: vendors depositing checks twice, checks stolen, checks forged and deposited in banks two states away, an internal employee writing checks to friends for "work completed," among many others. It's better to spend the relatively short amount of time reconciling your books with the bank statement every month. Getting into this habit will make doing Bank Reconciliations easier as your business grows.

One important safety item: it is highly recommended the same person(s) who cut checks and makes payments are *not* also doing the bank recs. Employees writing checks to themselves is not unheard of, and separation of duties helps to avoid this type of fraud.

You can do a Bank Reconciliation by hand. Here's an example:

Example 9.1:

See below for the transactions that occurred in the Bank Account, taken from the General Ledger, for the period we are reconciling:

Date	Type	Payee	Description	Debit	Credit	Balance
1-Jan	Deposit	Deposit	Opening Deposit	$ 1,000		$ 1,000
2-Jan	Deposit	Deposit	Rent From Tenant	3,000		4,000
3-Jan	Check 101	Ray's Electric	Electrical Work		300	3,700
7-Jan	Online Pmt	Water Company	January Water Bill		500	3,200
9-Jan	Check 102	John's Landscaping Co	January Landscaping		200	3,000
12-Jan	Check 103	Gas Company	January Gas Bill		500	2,500
15-Jan	Online Pmt	ABC Advertising	"FOR RENT" Signs		300	2,200

And from the bank statement:

Beginning Balance	$ -
Deposits and Other Credits	$ 4,000.00
Checks and other Paid Items	$ (1,000.00)
Ending Balance	$ 3,000.00

Deposits	Date	Amount
	1-Jan	$ 1,000.00
	2-Jan	$ 3,000.00

Checks and other Paid Items		
ACH PMT TO WATER CO	8-Jan	$ 500.00
Check #101	10-Jan	$ 300.00
Check #102	15-Jan	$ 200.00

There are a couple of differences in the two reports, and these differences are what need to be reconciled. First, note the differences in the dates of the payments and deposits from the General Ledger Check Register and the Bank Statement. Check #101 to Ray's Electric was written on 1/3/XX, but the bank did not issue payment until 1/10/XX. This is due to timing differences, with the check written and mailed in 1/3/XX but not received and deposited by Ray's Electric until 1/10/XX.

We see the same issue with check #102 to John's Landscaping, as well as the two deposits. This is why it is important to keep an up-to-date Check Register, so checks that have been written, but have not cleared the bank account, will be known by you as the owner and property manager. You do not want to make a payment if there are checks outstanding and thus not enough money in your account to cover them.

Next, as you can see below, there are two payments that are on the General Ledger Check Register: check #103 for $500.00 and an Online Payment for $300.00 that are not found on the bank statement. This is because the payments were not processed by the time the bank prepared the statement as of 1/15/XX. So, while the General Ledger Check Register shows a balance of $2,200, which is the most up-to-date balance in your account, the bank statement was not aware of those charges at the time of the statement, hence the statement showing a balance of $3,000. So, by adding the $500 check #103 and $300 online payment to the $2,200 check register balance, we come up with the bank balance of $3,000.

	Ledger	Bank
End Balance	$2,200	$3,000
Missing Items	None	-500 Check #103
		-300 Online Payment
Reconciled Balance	$2,200	$2,200

As this can be somewhat confusing and time consuming at first, it is important to allocate enough time and resources to successfully perform Bank Reconciliations. If you use an accounting software, there will usually be a bank reconciliation feature, which makes doing bank recs much easier and quicker. Whether you choose to do your bank reconciliations by hand or use accounting software, the lesson here is to make a habit of doing your Bank Reconciliations once you get your monthly bank statement.

PART II

Property Ownership, Property Management and Working with Tenants and Vendors

This part of the book will be most useful to those starting out in property ownership and management, and/or planning on doing the bookkeeping yourself. It will also be quite useful to the new property management bookkeeper and accountant, as we will review all the integral pieces of running a successful property ownership and management company. I wish when I started out working in property management I had had a resource section like this, and so I've provided one for you to utilize.

CHAPTER 10

Property Types

There are three main property types where an owner would need property management: **Residential, Commercial** and **Industrial.** All three property types come with risks and rewards, as does any type of investment. It is important to realize these before you jump into ownership or management. Some will require more hands-on work, others less. There are benefits and drawbacks to each type of property. We will examine each in-depth in order for you to understand which may suit you best.

We will look at some real-life examples and stories of occurrences I have seen and been a part of in my career in property management accounting to help give you examples of possible risks and rewards. All three property types will have building and structural codes specific to their type, and it is very important to note what you will have to do as an owner or manager in regard to meeting building codes.

There are also mixed-use properties, which combine residential and commercial properties in the same building, often with commercial spaces on the lower levels and residential on upper levels. These types of properties come with their own pluses and minuses, but you can infer these from the following descriptions of residential and commercial/industrial properties, as they are the same but combined. Let's start with Residential properties, then move on to Commercial and Industrial.

CHAPTER 11

Residential Properties

These are homes or domiciles, whether they be single family residences, apartment buildings, condominiums, duplexes and the like. Typically, the renter will be an individual, couple or family, and it will be their home (or vacation) residence. As you will be owning/managing where someone actually lives, there may be an inclination to be "nicer" to these tenants, and each owner/manager will have to decide how they want to handle their tenants.

There is the least amount of profit to be made from residential properties for the ownership when compared to the other two property types. This can be due to multiple factors, some being rent controls, the availability of rental properties (or over-saturation of the market), the inability to remove tenants that are delinquent in their payments, the costs of upkeep versus the ability to charge higher rents, and other mitigating factors.

I knew of one owner that had properties in a cold weather climate, and for one period had to go to court monthly for delinquent tenants. They could not evict the tenants due to it being winter and thus lost thousands of dollars in income as well as the expense of lawyers. Another owner had a major issue evicting one tenant because they were a hoarder, and left thousands of dollars' worth of damage to the apartment when they vacated.

The benefits of residential properties are the simplicity of leases and owners can often manage the properties with minimal expense. They can be a good entry point for a new property owner just beginning in the field of property ownership. Many times owners can develop good relationships with tenants so they stay for long periods and thus reduce turnover and the need to restore the property before renting to a new tenant.

I assisted with the year-end accounting for many owners who owned a few residential rental properties, and the expense was minimal on their part, because there were not many expenses that they had to pay for, once the property was rented. In these single-family rentals, the tenants were usually responsible for utilities and simple maintenance (such as lawn care), so there were many months where the ownership collected rent and had no expense.

Property taxes are typically the largest expense of ownership in residential properties. I knew one property owner that had the same tenant in their rental house for twenty years. He had to do minimal work on the house and was able to pay off his mortgage simply based on rents collected. He established a good working relationship with the tenant so that rental increases were negotiated, and the tenant rarely complained, thus leading to a fruitful investment.

More recently I have seen a rise in residential rental properties for short-term or vacation rentals. These can be highly profitable as they can earn a (much) greater return on a per-night basis but come with their own set of possible issues. Expenses may be greater, for example cleaning and utilities, as short-term rentals usually do not care about leaving the lights on or taking hourlong showers or clogging the toilets.

Local municipalities are beginning to more strictly regulate short term vacation rentals, demanding stringent adherence to the maximum number of guests, reduced noise levels, and collection of accommodation taxes. I have also seen where municipalities will put restrictions on the amount of time a property may be rented for a short-term rental.

There is also the issue of not being able to rent the property at all, and that can depend on the popularity of the area (for example in the downtown of a major city compared to a vacation destination that only sees three months a year of popularity).

All told, residential properties are often where a property owner acquires their first rental property. Thus, it is of the utmost importance for them (and you reading) to understand what to expect and realize the profit potential as well as the potential drawbacks to owning and managing rental properties. If you choose to hire a company, the future chapter on Hiring a Property Management Company will be very helpful.

CHAPTER 12

Commercial and Industrial Properties

Commercial properties are those where business is conducted and oftentimes these businesses will sell directly to the public. **Industrial properties** are typically large warehouses that are used for the storage and subsequent shipping of goods, and some do sell to the public as well. As Commercial and Industrial properties have many more similarities than differences, we will review them both together.

Examples of Commercial Properties are office buildings, strip centers and malls, and many of these will be of mixed usage. As there are many different types of commercial properties, it is important to understand and consider the similarities and differences between each different type of commercial property.

There are a variety of tenants who rent each type of space. Some may be one-building rentals, where one tenant rents the entire building. Examples include a big box store or a fast-food chain restaurant. Many cities and towns have taller office buildings where commercial tenants rent spaces and may have office hours open to the public but may not. Sometimes you will see a food restaurant on the ground floor of an office building with private tenants renting the offices above. Regardless of the tenant type, they are all doing the same thing, selling something. Whether it is selling food, sporting goods, clothing, movie tickets, jewelry, phones, financial advice or real estate – every commercial business is selling something.

It is important to note that while Residential properties deal with where a person lives and thus can be subject to much more scrutiny when it comes time to evict a tenant, commercial and industrial tenancy does not have that issue. Whether dealing with large corporate tenants or "mom and pop" shops of sole proprietors, the law is much more on the side of ownership, in my experience. Having a strong lease will go much farther than compared to residential tenancy, and we will delve more into those in the next two chapters.

The benefits of commercial properties can be the potential for (much) higher rents than residential, the ability to share expenses among many tenants for shared areas (in the form of Common Area Maintenance, or CAM, which will be detailed in a later chapter) and the ability to choose tenants (in good economic times) – even having have them compete for rental spaces, thus bringing in more money to ownership.

Downsides can be a lack of tenants in poor economic times, neighboring commercial centers taking successful tenants away, major costs in building up or fixing up a space and not recovering those costs for many years, greater start-up expenses and occasional expensive repairs to a property (replacing roofs and parking lots for example).

Another benefit is the ease of having the tenant be responsible for "everything on their side of the door" – meaning once the tenant was handed the keys and had inspected the rental space, any costs that came about inside the rental space was their responsibility, so less time and money was spent on behalf of the owner.

Industrial tenants often worked like this, so that any issue with their rental building was the tenant's responsibility, and only outside the building was the responsibility of ownership. This made Industrial building owners have to spend much less time on worrying and fixing the tenant's rental and allowed them to concentrate on purchasing more property and thus growing their portfolio. However, because of this, profits were less in Industrial properties than Commercial properties.

This idea can be understood as: the more the owner was responsible, the greater potential for profit.

CHAPTER 13

Leases

A lease is a legal document between two parties, where one party provides a property and the other uses the property for an agreed upon fee. That is a bit technical, so to put it in layman's terms, a lease is a contract between a lessee/renter and lessor/owner for the rental of a property or piece of property. Usually, the higher the rental amount charged by the lessor, the more complex the lease.

Residential leases are the simplest. Many municipalities provide standard residential leasing forms that can be attained at the appropriate government office. These are a good choice to use, as you may need to use your lease in a legal eviction proceeding at some point and using the governmental form leaves less open to interpretation. Typical items include:

- The rental amount
- Address of rental location
- Any utilities that are included
- The amount of the security deposit
- The length of time, including the specific starting and ending dates, of the lease term
- Amount of renters insurance (if required)
- The consequences of late payment
- Detail of Rent Increases (usually annually)
- Any Home or Renters association dues

- Any covenants (usually renter-specific items)

Commercial and Industrial Leases are often very similar. The commercial lease typically being the most complex because Industrial leases, as mentioned in the prior chapter, are for renting an entire warehouse space, and thus less the landlord is typically responsible for, so there is less need for many covenants. Of course, this is not always true, but in general that has been my experience when reviewing industrial lease types when compared to commercial ones. All of the same items that are found on the residential leases will also be found here, along with many other covenants. Typical items include:

- The rental amount
- Any utilities that are included
- The amount of the security deposit
- The length of time, including the specific starting and ending dates, of the lease term
- Amount of renters insurance (if required)
- The consequences of late payment
- The size (in square footage) and the exact location of the rental space
- Detail of Rent Increases (usually annually)
- Any covenants (usually renter-specific items)

For any and all lease types: The above lists are by no means exhaustive ones, and any lease or contract that will be entered into should be reviewed by a lawyer that specializes in real estate rental agreements.

CHAPTER 14

Lease Types: All-in versus Triple-Net

All-in leases are most typical in residential leases and are understood to mean that the tenant's monthly rent consists of one number, which includes the rent, any shared utilities and other property expenses. Put more simply, all expenses are included in the Rental Amount. Let us look at an example.

Example 14.1:

Janet signs a lease, for two years, to rent an apartment for $500 a month. In her lease, Janet is responsible for the electric utility bill, meaning that she needs to contact the Electric Company and set up an account to pay them directly. However, all the other utilities are included in the $500 monthly amount, and any and all other fees are also included in that amount. Janet will pay $500 for every month her lease is in effect, with a 5% annual increase for the second year.

As a landlord, ensure you and your tenant understand what is, and what is not, included in their monthly payment amount. If the tenant is responsible for any utilities, schedule a date that you will turn off services and the tenant is responsible to begin incurring the charges in their name. Do these things, and be as clear as possible with your tenant to avoid confusion and other possible adverse issues, or confusion, in the future.

Triple-Net Leases include charges that the tenant is billed for (besides Rent) and they are: Common Area Maintenance, Taxes and Insurance. These are considered "pass-through" expenses, meaning that the owner/landlord pays the expenses upfront, and the tenant reimburses the owner/landlord. Typically, these expenses are estimated based on prior year costs, so a reconciliation is usually done at a later date. We will discuss this in detail in Chapter 18: Triple Net Reconciliations. These triple-net charges are billed on a pro-rata share, which is calculated by dividing the tenant space square footage by the total building square footage. Let us look at an example.

Example 14.2:

Jack is renting a space that has the size of 10,000 square feet. The total square footage of the building that Jack's rental space is located in is 100,000 square feet. Jack's portion of the Triple Net Charges are: 10,000 / 100,000 = 10%. Jack is responsible for 10% of the Triple Net Charges. As owner, you will bill Jack (and the rest of the tenants) based on this pro-rata share.

Example 14.3:

The property has received the annual Property Tax Bill for $60,000. Jack's pro-rate share is 10%, thus Jack's cost would be $60,000 x 10% = $6,000. Often this amount is divided by twelve to give a monthly invoice amount. $6,000 / 12 = $500 monthly charge to Jack. Common Area Maintenance and Insurance are calculated the same way. The annual CAM charge is $96,000 for the center, Jack's portion is 10% of that, or $9,600 per year. Divide that by 12 months in the year, which makes his monthly amount $800. The annual insurance charge is $15,000 for the center, and Jack's 10% is $1,500. We divide this by 12 to get his monthly amount due of $125.

Example 14.4:

Jack's rent is $5,000 per month, his Common Area Maintenance charge is $800, Taxes are $500, and insurance is $125. Here are the costs on Jack's monthly invoice:

Rent	$5,000
CAM	$800
Taxes	$500
Insurance	$125
Total Invoice	$6,425

In Commercial Real Estate the landlord or owner provides the space for a rental fee and then the tenant assumes all other expenses, which includes Triple Net Charges that are variable and thus can change based on the actual expenses. A lease should include the ability to reconcile the Triple-Net Charges. What this means is that the tenant will receive either a bill or credit based on the actual expense versus how much they were billed.

Depending on the lease terms there may be other charges that the tenant is billed for. A few examples are:

- Sign Fees – if you have a monument sign or pole sign where the tenant's name is advertised
- HVAC Maintenance plan – where you will send an HVAC technician to provide service and maintenance and charge the tenant a flat fee
- Late Fees – for when the tenant pays after the date the rent is due in the terms of the lease

There can be many other charges that are specific to your property. These are not considered Triple-Net charges per se, however may be added to the invoice. Let us look at an example.

Example 14.5:

Here is Jack's invoice, updated to include other charges that Jack agreed to, which was an HVAC maintenance plan for $25 per month, and his business' name on the pole sign for $50 per month:

Rent	$5,000
CAM	$800
Taxes	$500
Insurance	$125
Signage:	$50
HVAC:	$25
Total Invoice	$6,500

Remember to detail all other expenses in the Lease. Lastly, do not forget that Residential leases are almost always All-in leases and Commercial Leases are almost always Triple-Net. Industrial Leases can be either, depending on how the property is structured and how the lease is written.

CHAPTER 15

Invoicing and Statements

We already saw some sample billing sections of an invoice in the last chaper; if you have ever received an invoice for a good or service provided you are already familiar. Residential invoices (15.1) typically are not mailed or provided to the tenant, as the amount is the same every month and as such, straightforward. However, some tenants may want to receive a bill monthly, or you as the owner want to send a bill monthly. Next is a full sample Commercial Invoice (15.2) with Triple-Net Charges, which includes an Invoice number, the date generated, the due date and the tenant's address. Lastly is a sample Industrial Invoice (15.3). Per the lease terms, electrical and signage are additional expenses charged to the tenant, but all other expenses are part of the Rental Amount.

Example 15.1: Residential Invoice

Barrington Property Management

INVOICE

DATE: February 1st, 2023
INVOICE # 100

Bill To:
Jill Pepper
1234 Main Street, Apt 1A
Anywhere, USA 99999

DESCRIPTION	AMOUNT
Monthly Rent	$ 1,000.00
TOTAL	$ 1,000.00

Make all checks payable to Barrington Property Management

THANK YOU FOR YOUR BUSINESS!

Example 15.2: Commercial Invoice

Barrington Property Management

INVOICE

DATE: February 1st, 2023
INVOICE #: 101

Bill To:
Jack's ABC Company
200 Main Street
Anywhere, USA 99999

DESCRIPTION	AMOUNT
Rent	$5,000
CAM	$800
Taxes	$500
Insurance	$125
Signage	$50
HVAC	$25
TOTAL	**$ 6,500.00**

Make all checks payable to Barrington Property Management

THANK YOU FOR YOUR BUSINESS!

Example 15.3: Industrial Invoice

Barrington Property Management   INVOICE

DATE: February 1st, 2023
INVOICE #: 102

Bill To:
XYZ Corp.
1007 Main Street
Anywhere, USA 99999

DESCRIPTION	AMOUNT
Rent	$15,000
Signage	$250
Electrical Utility Reimbursement	$250
TOTAL	$ 15,500.00

Make all checks payable to Barrington Property Management

THANK YOU FOR YOUR BUSINESS!

A **statement** is a summary of invoices due, and payments made, over a period of time and is used to summarize the amount the tenant owes to the owner. The period of time usually begins with the last invoice the tenant received and ends with the date the statement is mailed. You may have a tenant request all their rent payments for a year, or for a certain period of time, as well.

Often a statement is sent when a tenant is late on their rent, but may be sent when a reconciliation is done, or if the owner paid an expense on behalf of the tenant. It will also include any payments made in the timeframe of the statement. Let us look at an example.

Example 15.4:

The Industrial Tenant, XYZ Corporation, partially paid their rent after the five-day grace period as dictated by their lease for the prior month, and thus incurred a 10% late fee. This statement is dated 2/10/XX, and includes the prior month invoice amount, the payment made by the tenant, the late fee, and the current invoice amount, to determine the total balance due.

Barrington Property Management

Statement

DATE: February 10th, 20XX

Bill To:
XYZ Corp.
1007 Main Street
Anywhere, USA 99999

Date	DESCRIPTION	AMOUNT
	Balance Forward:	$3,500
2/1/20XX	Invoice #102	$15,500
2/5/20XX	Late Fee	$ 1,550.00
2/6/20XX	Partial Payment Check #1002	($10,000)
	TOTAL DUE IMMEDIATELY	$ 10,550.00

Make all checks payable to Barrington Property Management

THANK YOU FOR YOUR BUSINESS!

CHAPTER 16

Common Area Maintenance (CAM) and HOA Dues

Common Area Maintenance or CAM, for short, deserves its own chapter because it is that important to owning and managing a successful Commercial or Industrial property. CAM expenses are those expenses incurred that are for the benefit of all tenants of the property. These expenses that usually fall into CAM are: shared utilities, parking lot maintenance, fountain maintenance, cleaning of common areas, snow removal, hallway painting, landscaping, security, parking lot lights, pest control in common areas – among many others. The exact CAM charges will be specific to each property.

It is integral to differentiate between charges for Single tenant spaces, compared to charges for All tenant spaces. Depending on lease terms, an owner may perform work in one tenant space that is for the benefit of that one tenant. This charge would thus not be a part of common area maintenance for the property. Contrast that with painting the interior hallway of the office building annually. That is for the benefit of all the tenants, and thus would be a part of CAM. It is very important to track these charges separately, as later CAM reconciliations require tenants to be billed only for shared expenses.

The lease will dictate what charges are part of CAM for each tenant. That is why it may be easier to start with a boilerplate lease with standard charges included in CAM to begin with, and then these can be adjusted during the lease negotiations as necessary. I have seen some tenants that have their own trash service, since they generate a lot of trash and thus ownership did not want to incur the extra costs on behalf of the other tenants. Let's look at an example.

Example 16.1:

You own a strip center that has three tenants: one a restaurant which controls two-thirds of the center, and the other one-third is split between a nail salon and a jewelry store. Since the restaurant creates a lot more trash than a jewelry store or nail salon, you decided the restaurant needs to have their own dedicated trash dumpster, while the rest of the tenants at the property share one dumpster. So, the other tenants will share the trash charge for their shared dumpster, and the restaurant will have the charge for their exclusive trash dumpster. I saw this multiple times at centers, as most have a restaurant. You cannot charge the other tenants for the restaurant trash dumpster, or vice versa.

As we have mentioned previously, each tenant is responsible for their pro-rata share (which is typically calculated by taking the square footage of rental space and dividing that by the total building/property square footage). Let us look at an example.

Example 16.2:

Tenant One square footage is 1,000 square feet, and the total building square footage is 10,000 square feet. 1,000 / 10,000 = 10%. Thus, Tenant One has a pro-rata share of 10% of the shared expenses.

CAM is such an important part of renting and owning Commercial and Industrial Real Estate we are going to restate it: the common theme is these are all expenses incurred on behalf of all the tenants. You may hear (or say) the term "bill it back to the tenants" as I distinctly remember my first boss telling me this often, and then heard it from every subsequent property owner, manager or client I worked with. This most often relates to CAM and means add the expense in question to the shared CAM ledger for all the tenants (or bill it to the individual tenant, depending on if it was a CAM expense or not).

As a residential property owner, CAM isn't going to be billed out as such, but you still need to track the expenses of maintaining the property, including landscaping and snow removal, maintenance of shared common areas, walkways and parking lots. Tracking these costs will allow you to set and raise rents accordingly.

For residential properties located in a community, you may have Home Owner Association (HOA) dues, which are charges shared by all Home Owners in the community. These are similar to CAM, but simpler. Shared landscaping, gated security, a shared pool, clubhouse maintenance, and a host of other expenses can be rolled up into HOA dues. As the owner, you may decide to include these expenses in the total rental amount, pay them yourself or bill your tenant separately for them. Usually in the community your property is located in these fees are fixed and cannot be negotiated but ensure that you as the owner are not paying more than you should.

CHAPTER 17

Determining Correct amounts for Triple Net Charges

The easiest way to determine what amounts to bill tenants for triple-net charges is to look at the prior year expenses for Common Area Maintenance (CAM), property taxes and insurance. Many owners will add 5-10% to the prior year expense amount, figuring those expenses go up year after year, which they typically do. In my experience, it is much easier to refund money to tenants when you have over-collected than collecting from them later, so giving yourself as the owner a bit of "padding" can make reconciliations much easier (and your tenants happier when they receive a credit on their statement).

If you already have the prior year expenses for CAM, property taxes and insurance, you can skip ahead to the next chapter. However, let us say you have recently purchased a property or even built a new property. How do you determine Triple Net charges in the first year of the building?

Property Taxes are the easiest to determine, as there is one amount of the property taxes paid the year before, and this can be used as the basis amount to bill the tenants. Insurance should also be simple, as ownership will need to have a policy in place before tenants can take occupancy, so there will be a direct amount to be paid to the Insurance Company, which usually billed once or twice in a calendar year. Common Area Maintenance will be the most difficult to reconcile, as there are many, many charges that make up CAM, as has been previously discussed.

First, you as the owner/manager will determine the expenses you want to be part of CAM. These should be detailed in the lease, and the preceding chapter has a solid list of basic CAM charges. Next, call vendors and utility providers. Some of these providers you will have a contract with, for example, landscaping and trash pickup. So, you will know these expenses. However, utilities and other expenses may have to be estimated using the information available to ownership at the time.

With that being said, it's integral to ensure there is language in the lease that addresses the fact that this is a new (or renovated) property and thus CAM charges are estimated but are not able to be based on prior expenses, as they do not exist. As such, CAM may be undercharged and a CAM reconciliation will be performed after the first year, and the tenant will be responsible for any under-collection to be paid in a specified timeframe after the tenant receives the reconciliation invoice.

I worked for an ownership group that built an entirely new commercial center, and their five tenants were all national chains that many would easily recognize. Each tenant signed a fifteen-year lease, so the owners were very excited about having long-term, successful tenants that would be there a long time, so that consistent income would be generated from the property. Their mistake was that they neglected one major issue, and that was not putting language into the leases that would allow them to reconcile CAM based on the building being new, as they obviously did not know what the actual CAM charges would be.

They did their due diligence on taxes and insurance but vastly underestimated CAM. These major tenants had negotiated a maximum of 10% CAM increase every year and that would be the maximum due upon reconciliation for the prior year as well. When I did their accounting, they were under billing the CAM charges by thousands of dollars and due to the lease language, there was nothing they could do about it and this would continue for the 15-year lease term. As such this reduced their profits substantially.

CHAPTER 18

Triple Net Reconciliations

Why do we need to reconcile Triple Net Charges? One, the lease may (and should) call for it, in which case there will be verbiage that details how and when a Triple Net reconciliation is to be completed. A second reason is that neither the tenant or landlord want to be responsible for any more than their share of these pass-through expenses. Also remember that Triple Net charges are estimates, either based on prior expenses or based on a formulaic calculation, so performing a reconciliation will reconcile these estimated charges with the actual expenses incurred.

Performing a Triple Net reconciliation is as simple as the tenant leases involved. If all the tenants have the same lease language, then it is easy to figure out what the tenants owe. Let's look at a simple example.

Example 18.1:

You estimate the property tax bill for your center to be $60,000 based on the prior year expense. As taxes usually go up every year, the actual bill received was $65,000. Tenant One occupies 10% of the building in a commercial center. Tenant One paid $6,000 for property taxes in the prior year.

The increase means that Tenant One owes his pro-rata share of the $5,000 difference ($65,000 actual bill vs $60,000 estimated bill) to you ($5,000 x 10% = $500 Tenant One's share).

As the owner you will bill every tenant based on their pro-rata share and further based on the actual bill amount. It will work the same way for insurance. Insurance and Property Tax are straightforward reconciliations.

CAM can also be straightforward, however, often there are more caveats to it. CAM Reconciliations can become more cumbersome when there are caps or limits on the amount that can be charged for CAM, or even a specific CAM expense. CAM needs to be calculated based on all the Common Area expenses, of which there are typically many, and are billed at different times based on the specific expense. We will go into more detail in the next chapter.

As an owner, you will specify in the lease how often you will do these Triple-Net reconciliations, which I recommend performing once a year at minimum. You want to stay on top of these because, as the owner, you do not want to pay for more than your fair share. This is why you have a lease, and why the tenant has agreed to it.

Best practices dictate doing a reconciliation once a year and is easiest done on the calendar year basis (but you can choose any date you prefer). In my experience doing reconciliations in January usually ensures faster payment as Commercial and Industrial tenants usually make more money in December and thus have more funds in which to pay what they owe, quicker, and without hassle.

A prior company I worked for had put off doing Triple-Net reconciliations for more than three years when I came aboard, so that was the first thing I did as their new accountant. We recovered thousands of back owed monies, but as some tenants had moved out in those three years, we were unable to recover all that was due, and thus ownership lost money that they were owed. Of course, after that, we did them annually and ownership was never again unpaid for expenses they incurred on behalf of the tenant. Next, let us look at a sample invoice that details a triple net reconciliation for the prior year.

Example 18.2:

Barrington Property Management   **Invoice**

DATE: February 1, 20XX

Bill To:
XYZ Corp.
1007 Main Street
Anywhere, USA 99999

DESCRIPTION	AMOUNT
Amount **Collected** for Pro-Rata **Insurance** for the period of 1/1/X8-12/31/X8	(5,000)
Amount **Due** for Pro-Rata **Insurance** for the period of 1/1/X8-12/31/X8	5,300
Amount **Collected** for Pro-Rata **Property Taxes** for the period of 1/1/X8-12/31/X8	(1,200)
Amount **Due** for Pro-Rata **Property Taxes** for the period of 1/1/X8-12/31/X8	1,000
Amount **Collected** for Pro-Rata **CAM** for the period of 1/1/X8-12/31/X8	(3,000)
Amount **Due** for Pro-Rata **CAM** for the period of 1/1/X8-12/31/X8	3,400
TOTAL DUE IMMEDIATELY	$ 500.00

Make all checks payable to Barrington Property Management

THANK YOU FOR YOUR BUSINESS!

In the above example, the landlord underestimated the Insurance Charge by $300 ($5,000-$5,300), overestimated the property taxes charge by $200 ($1,200-$1,000) and underestimated the CAM charge by $400 ($3,400-$3,000). The equation to determine what the tenant owes to the landlord is: -$300 + $200 - $400 = $500. So, the tenant owes the landlord $500. Many tenants will want a Triple-Net reconciliation because they feel they may be overcharged by the owner, but it also protects the owner in case they have underbilled the tenant. I have seen the amounts go both ways, so it is good practice to know how to perform them to ensure no money is left on the table.

CHAPTER 19

CAM Recording Correctly to Make Reconciliations

Billing Common Area Maintenance, as mentioned in the prior chapter, is the hardest of the Triple-Net charges to estimate. Beneficially, once you have owned the property for a year or more, you can get a better understanding of what to accurately charge for CAM. The most important factor of keeping a CAM reconciliation easiest is to track CAM expenses correctly. Ensure you, your staff, or your property management company has a full understanding of the expenses that can go into CAM and what cannot. Again, this is determined by the lease.

When I was leading the accounting department at a large property management firm, I created two different account groupings, one called CAM Expenses and the other Non-CAM Expenses (obviously very technical terms, but I believe in keeping it simple). Meaning, could we recover these charges from all the tenants through CAM, or not. In keeping it simple I created different account numbers for CAM and Non-CAM expenses. In this case, every account number that started with a 6 (six) would be CAM Expenses, and every Non-CAM Expense account would begin with a 7 (seven). Each expense type would have a different CAM Expense and Non-CAM Expense account number. Let us look at a few examples so you can see what I mean, and thus put into practice for yourself.

Example 19.1:

6100 Landscaping CAM
7100 Landscaping Non-CAM
6200 Electric Utility CAM
7200 Electric Utility Non-CAM
6300 Legal Fees CAM
7300 Legal Fees Non-CAM

Furthermore, I would advise all new employees of the easiest way to understand if the expense they had was a CAM or Non-CAM charge. If there is a question, think of this: *Can we bill the tenants for this charge?* If so, choose the corresponding CAM account, if not, choose the Non-CAM Account. Here are a few examples.

Example 19.2:
We pay landscaping for the whole property and thus can bill the tenants for this charge. That is 6100 Landscaping CAM Expense.

Example 19.3:
We pay for the shared building electric. That is a 6200 Electric Utility Expense. We pay the electricity to keep the lights on in a vacant space, so that when we show it, we can turn the lights on. That is 7200 Non-CAM Electric Utility Expense.

Example 19.4:
We pay a lawyer to sue a bad tenant; that is not a charge shared by ALL tenants, and as such would be 7300 Legal Fees Non-CAM Expense.

When we arrived at the year end and the time to do CAM reconciliations, it was much simpler to complete them. Of course, there were exceptions as mentioned prior, however because we started knowing all the CAM charges, it was easy to remove the exceptions and proceed with finishing the reconciliations. To reiterate, it is most important to track all CAM expenses correctly and thoroughly. Ensure you and your team know what can and is a part of CAM and what cannot be, to save time and money.

CHAPTER 20

Rent Rolls

A rent roll is a list of the tenants of a property and often includes: their address, square footage of rental space, monthly charges, lease start and expiration, renewal date, base rent increase date, and other pertinent items. Typically rent rolls are updated monthly but can be updated at the discretion of ownership. Rent rolls can be used to assist in performing Triple Net Reconciliations, as well as keep ownership and management abreast of tenant lease expiration's, rent increases, and the like.

They can be used by ownership to see the status of their property at a glance and to ensure charges on the invoices match the lease. Rent rolls also help your leasing agents know comparison prices when looking for new tenants and be kept abreast of future lease renewal dates. Ensure that your rent rolls are kept in a safe space or stored on a secure computer, as if your competition can gain access to them, they can undercut your rental rates. Most every company, property owner, and management company were very protective of their rent rolls, with good reason.

In my experience it took very little time to update rent rolls monthly. At one of my prior commercial property management companies, we updated the rent rolls monthly and this was of great assistance to our leasing agents as they had the most up to date information to use to negotiate leases with new tenants. But I also had residential clients that only updated their rent rolls once or twice a year, because they did rent increases on an annual basis. How up-to-date a rent roll is can be best determined by how important it is to have timely information for ownership and leasing purposes.

The most in-depth rent roll is for commercial real estate, as that will have the most amount of expenses found on it. Industrial will be similar, and the most basic is residential. To follow is a Commercial Rent Roll for one building with multiple addresses containing pertinent items typically found on a rent roll; however, you can add or remove items to fit your specific property. Let us look at an example with an explanation of each column to follow.

Example 20.1:

PB Property Management Group
Rent Roll for Commerical Property #1
Property Address: 123-135 Main Street
Month/Year: July

1	2	3	4	5	6	7	8	10
Address	Tenant Name	Square Footage	Base Rent	CAM	Taxes	Insurance	Sign Fee	Total
123 Main	Bob's Tax Service	1000	$ 2,000	$ 1,000	$ 625	$ 250	$ 200	$ 4,075
125 Main	XYZ Plumbers	1000	$ 2,500	$ 1,250	$ 781	$ 313	$ 200	$ 5,044
127 Main	VACANT							
129 Main	Gary's Lamp Emporium	2000	$ 4,500	$ 2,250	$ 1,406	$ 563	$ 200	$ 8,919
131-135 Main	Rugs and More	3000	$ 7,000	$ 3,500	$ 2,188	$ 875	$ 200	$13,763
Total:		7000	$ 16,000	$ 8,000	$ 5,000	$ 2,000	$ 800	$31,800

1	2	11	12	13	14	15
Address	Tenant Name	Lease Start	Lease End	Rent Increase	Rent Increase Terms	Lease Renewal?
123 Main	Bob's Tax Service	5/1/X5	5/1/X9	May	3% of Base Rent	1; 3 year option
125 Main	XYZ Plumbers	1/1/X1	M2M	January	$200	None
127 Main	VACANT					
129 Main	Gary's Lamp Emporium	3/1/X2	3/1/X9	March	5% of Base	2; 5 year option
131-135 Main	Rugs and More	11/1/X5		November	$500	None

THE BARRINGTON GUIDE TO PROPERTY MANAGEMENT ACCOUNTING

First (1) column	Address of Rental
Second (2) column	Tenant Name
Third (3) Column	Square Footage (this should match the lease)
Fourth (4) Column	Base Rent Amount (this should be directly from the lease)
Fifth (5) Column	CAM (This is a calculated amount based on the tenant's square footage)
Sixth (6) Column	Taxes (This is a calculated amount based on the tenant's square footage)
Seventh (7) Column	Insurance (This is a calculated amount based on the tenant's square footage)
Eighth (8) Column	Sign Fee (This is an Additional Expense specific to the tenant; you may want to add more columns if you have more monthly fees)
Ninth (9) Column	Total Amount = adding together the amounts in Columns 4-8
Tenth (10) Column	Lease Start Date
Eleventh (11) Column	Lease End Date (M2M = Month to Month, meaning the lease has expired)
Twelfth (12) Column	Rent Increase Month; the month the base rent will increase
Thirteenth (13) Column	Rent Increase Terms: By what means the rent will increase. Sometimes this will be a percentage, taking the current base rent and multiplying that by a percentage amount set in the lease; or an amount set in the lease. For the first tenant, their rent will increase by 3% (the equation for renewal base rent amount = Current Base Rent + Current Base Rent x 3%)
Fourteenth(14) Column	If the Lease has the option for a lease renewal, the number of options, and the amount of time of the option. For the first tenant, they have one lease option for three years

PART III

The Professionals: Assembling your Team and Choosing a Property Manager

Deciding to hire a property manager or manage it yourself is the first decision after acquiring a property, and we will look at both options so you can decide which is best for you. Finding the right team of professionals to assist with your property ownership will make success much easier in your property ownership endeavors. This part will ensure you have necessary information to hire and enlist the best professionals to help you achieve your goals. It will also assist in preparing 1099s for your vendors.

CHAPTER 21

Hire a Property Management Co or Manage Yourself

This may be your first property (if so, congratulations!) or your 10th property or your 100th. Regardless, you must choose how you want to manage it. Your choices hereon will determine how successful you are in property ownership. There are no absolutes when choosing whether to hire a property manager or property management company and as such, there will always be exceptions as every property is different. When deciding whether to hire a property management company, review the following options:

Price. Can you afford to hire *this* property manager or property management company? They typically charge a percentage of the gross rents. Compare rates and experience.

Knowledge of your industry. Does the company work mainly with the type of property you have? You do not want a company with residential-only experience managing your strip center, and vice versa. Experience working with your specific type of property is a key factor when choosing a property manager or property management company.

How much **assistance** do you need? Many property management companies will also provide leasing agents, who will find tenants for your property, and if this is something you are interested in, make sure the company you hire does it.

How **close**, in physical proximity, are you to your property? If you live in another state, or a faraway city, how will you ensure that your property is looked after? If you are in the same city or town, it is usually easier to keep on top of happenings at your property, but if you live far away that becomes more difficult, and you may have to utilize a property manager.

CHAPTER 22

Managing it Yourself

Being your own property manager is most easily done if you do not have a full-time job, but that depends on the type and size of the property, of course. If you have one single-family home you are renting, most likely there are not going to be many, if any, day-to-day issues, and calling professionals like plumbers, electricians, and the like are enough to handle most issues. If you choose to manage yourself, allocating enough time is key. You should be able to determine how much time you are spending on your property after a couple of months. If it is more time than you can handle, it may be time to hire a property management company.

For most of us, managing more than a few single-family homes or duplexes, an apartment building or two, a small strip center, or a couple industrial buildings, would be a full-time job in and of itself. If you choose to go this route, make sure you are ready for the challenge, but have faith in yourself you will be able to manage them (and this book will help!).

Each rental space, regardless of the industry, will have issues unique unto itself. I remember one week we had a roof leak in one space, an electric service panel blew at another space, an A-Coil had to be replaced in an HVAC system for another tenant, and the parking lot was getting re-striped, all at the same center. It was an intense management week at the building, to be certain, but we had a team in place to handle it effectively.

Be sure to recognize that the degree of difficulty increases the more properties you manage. Many owners start with one property, and figure out how to manage it, and then go forward and acquire more. As this happens, you will develop relationships with vendors, from landscapers to plumbers to HVAC technicians to roofers, and you will find creating this network invaluable. Equate it to when you find the perfect, trustworthy car mechanic.

Having a dedicated network of trusted professionals will assist in all aspects of a property, from acquisition (legal documents, inspections, etc.) to managing. As more properties are acquired, it may become time to start your own property management company and hire employees to manage your growing property empire!

CHAPTER 23

Hiring a Property Management Company

As an owner, you may not want to manage the properties you own yourself and would rather hire a property management company to do the job. I have worked for and with many property management companies, so I have been able to witness what both sides expect and will do regarding a property. As such, I can recommend as a property owner what you should be looking for in a property management company.

There are a few different types of property management companies, usually broken down by size. Some companies are local, others regional and then the big ones cover the entire nation. First, locate a few that operate in your area. You can use the internet, but many times in the neighborhood your property is in, you will see management company signs. Ask your friends and colleagues that are also property owners who they use. Next, call the management companies. If they are available when you call, that is a good sign. If they call you back within 24 hours that is also a good sign. If they do not, then I would not consider them.

Proceed using the same modus operandi when choosing any vendor; seek out three and compare and contrast. You will enter into a contract with the management company, and you can dictate and negotiate many of the terms of the contract. Here are a few points that you should ensure you understand and ask about before hiring a property management company.

Confirm their management fee (or rate): Usually the rate they will charge you to manage your property is based on monthly income, often 10% of the collected rent (which is referred to as Gross Income). Make sure you are very clear on "Collected" Rent (meaning Cash Basis). I have seen where property management companies collect on Accrual Rent, meaning they get their management fee regardless of if the tenant pays, because the tenant was billed.

You want to avoid any company that collects their fees like this. However, you can also negotiate this, and there may be some wiggle room as I have seen some property management companies that charge as much as 15% and others charge as low as 8%. It is key to do your homework and compare.

You may also negotiate that their management fee is based on Net Income, which is the property's Gross Income, minus its expenses. This can be good and bad. It can encourage the property management company to keep expenses low, but you do not want them to neglect the property in order to do so. In my experience using the Gross collected income is usually the way to go, and what most property management companies prefer, but remember, it is up to you.

What they will do for you: Never assume what the property management company will do. The contract should detail what exactly they will be required to perform to manage your property. For example, let us say they will collect the rents from your tenants by the fifth of the month (as stated in the lease you have agreed to with your tenants). After that date, the rent is late and the property managers will visit the tenant, and after the tenth day they will send a letter to the tenant informing them of the delinquency. This way you do not have to worry about your tenants getting behind on their rent and nothing being done about it. Furthermore, ensure they understand the leases you already have with your tenants.

Inquire and determine how much, and the frequency, of common area work there is to be done, including landscaping, cleaning and the like, as well as who will be performing CAM reconciliations and how frequently they will be performed. You may determine a dollar amount that, as long as the expense is less than that, then the property management company will hire the correct vendor to perform the work. I worked with one owner who authorized any expense under $500, another owner of more properties had a threshold of $2,000 and a third used $10,000 as their authorization limit.

Some property management companies will also be **leasing agents**, or have a leasing arm of their business, and can thus attain new tenants for your property. Alternatively, you may want to use another leasing agent to bring in new tenants, or use both options. For the latter two options, ensure the property management company knows this before you enter into the agreement. It is always best to have as many potential tenants as possible looking at your property, so then you can choose the best fit.

Preferred Vendors: Property Management companies have their own preferred vendors as they can attain discounts for supplying said vendor with a lot of work, including work generated by your property. As such, they may be averse to using your vendor. That is fine, as long as you understand the rate. Also, you may have a landscaper who has already been working on your property and want to keep them. If so, make sure that is clear in the contract.

Right to Cancel: Of course, you want the relationship to work out between you and your new Property management company. However, to protect yourself if things are just not working out, you should ensure you can cancel the contract. A good timeframe is six months.

What date they will supply your Financial Reports: I worked for an ownership group who owned many properties and utilized different property management companies because the properties were located all over the country. We needed the reports for the prior month by the 10th of the current month, to ensure I could review, make any necessary adjustments, and provide consolidated reports to the ownership group by the 15th.

In the contract with the different property management companies, it was written that we would receive the reports by the 10th. This was occasionally contentious as some of the companies were used to reporting by the end of the current month, and thus we had our internal bookkeeper's follow-up with these property management companies on the 8th of every month, to ensure we received the reports in the agreed upon timeframe.

Review the monthly reports: Property management companies will provide long and dense monthly reports. I believe this is done because they do not want ownership digging into the details of the monthly reports as a busy owner most likely does not have the time to review a 50-page monthly report in depth, every month. So, I recommend you review a few reports, and then be prepared to ask questions, if you have any, about these reports.

You want to review your Profit and Loss Statement, Accounts Receivable Aging Report, and the General Ledger. The Profit and Loss Statement will provide a lot of information about your income and expenses for the month, and you can also see how the company calculated their fee. The Accounts Receivable Aging Report will tell you which tenants are behind in their payments, and for how long. The General Ledger will show you any expenses that seem out-of-the-ordinary.

As you begin your relationship with the property management company, reviewing the first few months of reports are key to the success of your property. Spend the time, because once you, as the owner, understand how and why the property management company is managing your property in the way they do, you can decide if it is worth it to stay with them, choose another company to manage, or manage it yourself.

The Property Management Company is like any other vendor; they work for you, and they do that for pay. They do not own the property as you do, and you should never assume they will take as much care or diligence in taking care of your property and collecting rents from the tenants, as you, the owner, would.

Another company I worked for had staff whose job it was to confirm and check that the work that the property management companies said was being done was actually being done. With all that being said, you should be reasonable but clear in your expectations of the property management company should you decide on using one.

CHAPTER 24

Leasing Agents, Brokers, and Real Estate Lawyers

While Leasing Agents and Brokers will provide similar services, how they are compensated and by whom should be determined before entering any lease agreement. Usually, an agent or broker will bring a prospective tenant to your attention, and they are tasked with working out the details of the lease with you, instead of you working with the tenant directly.

This can be beneficial because, as professionals, these Agents and Brokers want to ensure both parties are happy as it is financially beneficial to them (which is a great motivator). If they work well with you, they may bring you other tenants, and if they do a good job for the tenant, said tenant will tell other prospective business owners.

The downside is having to pay the Agent or Broker a commission, and if you have to pay it all up front and the tenant defaults or moves out before the end of the lease term, you can (usually) not recuperate this from the Agent or Broker.

One company I worked for would have an agreement with the Agent or Broker that if the tenant was still in good standing, they would pay them annually for the commission, which was the entire commission divided by the years of the lease. This worked well for the owner because then the Agent or Broker was motivated to bring better quality tenants to the owner. Let's look at an example.

Example 24.1:

A tenant signed a five-year lease at $1,000 a month. The owner and leasing agent agreed to pay the agent one month of rent for each year of the lease. The owner agreed to pay the leasing agent $1,000 when signing the lease, and $1,000 on that anniversary annually, if the tenant was still occupying the rental space, for a total of $5,000.

The Agent or Broker will often use a standard lease provided by their company and if this is your first property you may want to utilize their standard lease. It also gives you a template to tweak as you see fit. Maybe you want to provide HVAC Maintenance as a separate expense (which I recommend, because in my experience tenants do not keep up the HVAC as well as you will) or maybe the standard lease does not require a personal guarantee and that is something you require. Make sure you can edit the lease to fit your needs. Also, you can utilize addendums to add any additional items you want to include in the lease agreement.

If the tenant signs a lease that was brought to you by a Leasing Agent or Real Estate Broker, they may have an agreement to pay the Agent or Broker, and these fees are negotiated between them and the tenant. You will also receive a bill from the leasing agent if you entered into an agreement with said Agent or Broker. All of this should be detailed in the lease, so there is no confusion later.

Always have a REAL ESTATE lawyer review the lease. I capitalized real estate because you want a lawyer that specializes in the field. Do not ask your friend who is a prosecutor, or your friend that works in patent law; they are not specialists. Find one that is and work out the price upfront for lease reviews. More than likely, you will use your first lease as a template for others.

Best practices state that as a building owner you want to provide the lease that the tenant will sign, not the other way around. However, some national tenants will make you sign *their* lease; in which case you definitely want a lawyer to review and, as a bonus, you may also pick up some verbiage from their lease that you can use later in your own leases.

Another great benefit of establishing who your legal representation will be is that they can do other things for you. For example, they can send the tenant a notice if the tenant is not paying the rent and they can also represent you in court in the case of tenant evictions. Having a good real estate lawyer that you trust is key to good property ownership and management.

CHAPTER 25

Hiring Contractors and Choosing Vendors

As an owner managing the property yourself, you will need a good team of contractors and vendors to help you do this. For example: plumbers, landscapers, electricians, HVAC technicians, handymen, roofers, trash haulers, among others that may be more specific to your property. It is possible that, if you are a homeowner, you may have some of these vendors at the ready, which is an excellent start.

For some expenses, a maintenance contract may need to be signed. Examples of this are weekly trash pickup, timely HVAC inspections and filter replacements, landscaping, etc. When choosing a vendor for recurring work, inspect the contract very carefully. A lawyer (most likely) is not necessary, but if you have one that specializes in contracts, you could have them review. Also, the terms of the contract should allow for cancellation at any time, as well as specify rates, if and when the rate could be increased, the frequency of the work to be done, and anything that is important to you as the manager/owner of the property.

Lastly, if possible, find a competent handyperson. They should be able to do minor fixes on most things but also know when to call in an expert if necessary. They also usually come at a lower rate than an expert and depending on their capabilities they can save a manager/owner a lot of money, worry and time.

At every property management firm I worked for and every property-owning client I worked for there was a dedicated handyperson.

This person was used for a whole host of jobs, from managing buildouts and capital improvements to minor electrical fixes to monitoring the laundry room to meeting other technicians and checking their work or meeting with inspectors from the local government agencies. Trust is the most important factor when finding a dedicated handyperson in my experience, but once an owner found a good one, they never let them go. Trust works for the handyperson as well, as a trusting relationship will lead to more work and thus more money for them.

Whether you have one property or many, you will have to insure the property, and this will lead you to an insurance agent. You can usually find many commercial property insurance agents that will specialize in this field, and it is important and best practices to interview a few and have them give you bids to insure your properties. It is very important to be upfront about your properties because that way there will be fewer, if any, issues if you must utilize your insurance.

Also, you will want to ensure you are covered exactly how you want to be. I knew one property owner that was very concerned with earthquake coverage because their properties were located near a fault line and was willing to pay more to ensure all their properties were covered. Another property owner I worked with, in a different area of the country, was the exact opposite, and did not feel earthquake coverage was necessary (even though most of the properties were located in an earthquake zone!). Each owner had their specific wants and needs, and their agents worked to give them a package that covered this, called a Binder. I had to read and review these policies and make sure all the bids received offered the same coverage, so I learned a lot about property insurance in my time as well, and it is dense, but good agents will provide summary pages to assist.

Something we, as individuals, are advised to do every couple of years (though many of us do not) is shop our car insurance. As a property owner/manager it is imperative to shop your property insurance every three years at minimum. I have worked with a variety of insurance agents, and not one was ever offended or hurt that we would take offers from other agents every couple of years. In a few cases we even changed agents and three years later returned to the prior agent, as they had the best rates at that time. As with any vendor, it pays to shop around.

Another important professional group to find is a service for lowering property tax bills. Many municipalities allow for the presentation of information to reduce the property tax bills on a property. These companies exist in most major markets and what they will do is research, and then go to the municipality your government is located in that controls the property tax, and negotiate on your behalf for a lower rate. Some municipalities will allow property taxes to be renegotiated every two years, others more and others less. The service will do this for a percentage of the reduction they are able to attain, so they are motivated to get you a reduction on your taxes. You can attempt to do this yourself, however it can be time consuming.

This can have two benefits for the owner. One is that, if you are a residential or industrial owner and the tenants are paying an all-in amount, you can reduce the property tax expense without having to reduce the amount of rent collected. For commercial owners, while insurance is a triple net charge that is reconcilable and thus the tenant will owe less, you can incorporate the expense of the reduction into CAM, as well as increasing goodwill with your tenants by reducing one of their triple net expenses.

CHAPTER 26

Choosing and working with a CPA

A Certified Public Accountants, or CPA for short, is an important member of your team since they will assist you in filing your taxes. I have worked with CPAs from the business owner side as well as worked for CPA firms throughout my career, and the benefits have been enormous. Seeing the working relationship from both sides allows me to bring new information and fill-in missing pieces easier and more efficiently.

The stories and examples I have used thus far have come from real life experiences, either working with clients on the CPA side or working for property owners on the other side. I was able to learn so much, and I want to share with you what I learned from both sides, so you can save time when choosing a CPA to assist you on your property ownership and/or management journey. I will also provide a few tips on how to keep your bills low and have your taxes filed on time.

It is likely you already have had a CPA prepare your personal taxes and you may very well have them handle your burgeoning property management business (but then again maybe not. Why? Read on). Maybe you have always used your local strip mall accounting firm to do your taxes, or even an online service, or you even do them yourself. If you do any of these for your personal taxes, that is excellent. However, make sure to find a CPA to prepare your business' taxes. The amount you pay your CPA will be deductible on your tax return, and also provides you a dedicated contact if/when you must deal with the IRS, among many other benefits.

If you have a dedicated CPA already, ask them if they do a lot of returns for Property Management Companies and their level of experience. A good CPA will tell you if they do or do not have experience in the field, and if not, they will direct you to a colleague more suited for your business needs. If you do not already have a CPA, you will need to find one. Ask your friends and business contacts; it is well known that many people choose based on word-of-mouth, which is fine. Do an internet search for CPAs in your area and add them to your list. You may also be familiar with some international CPA firms; however, they will usually cost you the most.

Next, make a list of a few CPAs you have found. Then call them. If they're available when you call, that's a good sign. If they call you back within 24 hours that's also a good sign. If they don't, then I wouldn't consider them. Once you have your CPA list, schedule a time to meet them in their office. That way you can use your human intuition skills and determine if they are the right fit for you. Ensure you speak with a Partner in the firm (or if a small firm, the Owner). Prepare to interview them and use the following tips as a guide:

Assess their experience working with property management firms. You want to hear them speak knowledgeably about Property Management, using terms mentioned in this book.

Inquire as to the size of their firm and how many partners, managers and staff. If you want one of the big ones with reputation and resources, go to them (but be prepared to pay their prices). I have found that a small-to-midsize firm works best for those just starting their Property Management business.

Ask their fees. If you tell them how many properties you own, and tell them about your income (or, even better, bring your prior year tax return with you) they should be able to give you a pretty fair estimate on what it costs to file your tax return.

As much as CPAs can be helpful on tax issues, they do have their limits. CPAs should never be treated as financial advisors, even though many CPA firms are also adding that to their company's repertoire. They will almost always recommend/advise for the most beneficial tax consequences, which may or may not be the best decisions for your business. As a business owner, you should take their advice into account, and definitely engage in tax planning as necessary, but do not treat their advice as gospel. You are running your property or property management company; the final decision always rests with you.

Lastly the CPA will make you sign an **engagement letter**. I encourage you to read this carefully, but to sum it up: it is basically a document that removes them from liability regarding your taxes. You must sign it to get them to perform the work for you, so see it as a necessary evil. If you feel after meeting and choosing your CPA that they are reputable and trustworthy, allow yourself peace of mind that although ultimately you are liable for your taxes, you have chosen a good CPA to work for your business.

Bonus Tip: Once you have chosen your CPA and they have prepared your tax return, review the Adjustments your CPA made to your books in order to file the tax return. This should be done before the tax return is filed. Your CPA will normally make adjustments to record Depreciation and Amortization, and they may also capitalize expenses. You will want to review these because I have seen CPAs capitalize expenses that should not have been, and ownership does not notice since they were not told. However, they will also assist in correcting bad bookkeeping as well, and that can be very helpful if you or your staff are inexperienced doing the bookkeeping yourself. Let's look at a real-life example.

Example 26.1:

I saw one CPA capitalize $26,000 of expense, because that was the total in the Repairs and Maintenance expense account at year end. This CPA just saw an expense on the Profit and Loss Statement for $26,000 and knew it was a large amount and capitalized it. Upon further review, that $26,000 was made up of 43 bills paid throughout the year totaling

$26,000, for normal, not capital, repairs. No one bill was more than $2,000, and many were much less. In that case, the CPA did not investigate further and thus cost the ownership an additional $26,000 of expenses they could have utilized on their tax return.

CHAPTER 27

Other Consultants

If you are planning on doing major repairs and/or improvements to your properties, you're most likely going to need other professionals (including engineers, architects, among others). If you hire a general contractor to perform the necessary work, they will most likely know of and/or utilize an engineer and/or architect.

If you are going to be your own General Contractor for your project you should find two or three local professionals, clearly present the project to them, and get a bid on the work before agreeing to work with them. For complex projects possibly have your lawyer review the contract; but for smaller jobs this may very well not be necessary.

If you cannot afford the property you want to purchase on your own, a loan may be necessary. You will need to find a loan officer, and if you have a personal home loan, you can start there. You should also talk to other loan officers, bankers, and credit unions to see who will give you the best interest rate, as well as most money. You can also look at private investors, and in that case your lawyer can assist with paperwork needed. If you choose to utilize private investors, note you will most likely have to prepare tax form K-1 for them, so make sure you keep your CPA in the loop if this is the route you choose.

CHAPTER 28

1099s

Now you have your vendor and professional team in place and have paid them for the work they do. After the calendar year ends, you will need to issue them a 1099 for the payments you have made to them in the previous calendar year. A 1099 is a tax form issued by an owner to a vendor for work performed in excess of $600. This applies to any vendor that is not a Corporation. Lawyers, even if a corporation, are required to get a 1099, and I will let you infer why. You can still choose to issue any vendor a 1099 for amounts paid under $600, but it is not required by the IRS (as of this writing). You will not issue a 1099 to any utility company in a majority of cases.

Any sole proprietor, individual, or LLC will be sent a 1099 after the tax year is completed. A federal tax identification number and address are furnished to ownership by the vendor on a form called a W-9 (Request for taxpayer Identification Number and Certification form). There are boxes to check for different entity types, and your vendor will check the appropriate box.

Best practices state that you should attain a W9 before you have any vendor start work, if for no other reason than it is much easier collecting it before you pay them than after, in my experience, and you do not want to be chasing a vendor at year end for their W9. A W9 form is a Request for Taxpayer Identification Number (Tax ID) and Certification. Note that a tax ID for a sole proprietor or individual is (often) their Social Security Number.

Let us look at a couple examples to see if and when to issue a 1099 to a vendor.

Example 28.1

You pay your electrician, Bob's Handy Electrical Services, $750 in total for the year. You attain a W9 from them, and they have a Tax ID and they checked the box to indicate they are an LLC. You will issue Bob's a 1099 for $750.

Example 28.2

You pay your trash service company, XYZ Garbage Hauling, Inc. $5,000 during the year. As they are a corporation, you will not issue them a 1099.

Example 28.3

You pay Bette's Copy Services LLC $200 to make "For Lease" signs for your property during the year. Since you paid Bette's less than $600 you are not required to issue a 1099 but can do so if you wish.

Example 28.4

You paid your lawyer $2,000 for reviewing leases during the year. You will issue him a 1099 for $2,000.

Note that there are fines associated with not sending a 1099 to a vendor that qualifies for one, and it is important to check with the IRS. You can order free 1099 forms and instructions from the IRS website (as of this writing). However, the onus is on the vendor to report correct earnings. It is always best practice to issue a 1099, even if you do not attain a W9 or Tax ID or Social Security number, to protect yourself and your property.

If you pay a vendor via a credit card, the credit card company will issue the vendor a 1099; you will not factor payments made via credit card into any 1099s you issue. Let us look at another example.

Example 28.5

you paid ABC Plumbing, LLC three times during the prior year. You paid them $500 by check and two times by credit card, for a total of

$1,500. You are not required to issue them a 1099, because your credit card company will issue them a 1099 for the $1,500 charge, and the $500 payment you made via check is below the $600 limit.

Alternately, let us say you paid them $1,000 via check, and $1,500 via credit card. You would issue the vendor a 1099 for $1,000. Separately, the credit card company would issue one for $1,500.

PART IV

In-Depth Accounting for Property Ownership and Management

This section will delve into more specific accounting details, in order for you to gain a greater grasp of some of the higher-level concepts and bookkeeping for property ownership and management. We will review the two Accounting Basis types; Fixed Assets; Depreciation and Amortization; Closing Statements; and how to record the sale of a property.

CHAPTER 29

Cash Basis and Accrual Basis Accounting

The Financial Statements for your company (as well as the Tax Return) can be prepared on one of two Accounting Basis types, named Cash Basis or Accrual Basis. This is an extremely important concept to grasp as it will affect all financial aspects of your property management or property-owning company. We will look at both options using more examples to help grasp the concepts. There is no right or wrong choice, however it is a choice that must be made.

It should be made before you begin your accounting, if at all possible, because you choose a basis to report your taxes on, which is why it is important. Choosing the correct Basis will also determine how you record revenue and expenses. We will also look at some comparative financial statements to show differences between the two to better assist you in choosing the correct basis for your property.

CHAPTER 30

Cash Basis Accounting

Cash Basis Accounting records transactions (revenue and expenses) when cash is either received or paid. It's that simple. Well, not *that* simple, but pretty simple. Let us dive into the specifics. First off, how you record Income, or Cash Into your bank account. The tenant pays you rent, and the day you receive payment from one of your tenants and deposit that payment into your bank is the day you record it as income. Let's look at an example:

Example 30.1:

Your tenant pays you $1,000 on the 30th of January for February Rent. So, on the 30th you take the check and deposit it in the bank, and you record the deposit (and income) on your books on the 30th. Thus, on your January Financial Statements, the $1,000 Rent the tenant paid you on January 30th (regardless of if it was for February Rent) is included in your **January** Reports.

It works the same way for expenses, or Cash paid out (to pay bills). Some vendors make you pay in advance for the future month, and some charge you for prior months. Regardless, when you actually make the payment is when you will record the expense. Let us look at another example:

Example 30.2:

You write a check to pay your Gas bill of $300 on the 30th of January for the first quarter (the period January to March). The check is deposited by the Gas Company on February 5th. The Gas Expense is recorded on the 30th, regardless of when the Gas Company deposited the check, because that is when you recorded the cash leaving your bank. (As we move away from check writing, this becomes even easier and even more applicable for Bank Transfers, ACH, EFT and wire transfers, as they occur on the same day).

Example 30.3:

You paid a landscaping service $900 for the first quarter of the year in advance, on January 2nd. Even though you paid them for three months' work, you will record the expense on the date you paid them, January 2nd, and the $900 expense will be found on your January financial statements.

Cash Basis seems pretty simple, right? When money comes in, you record it on your books as income (or inflow, if you like). When you send money out, you record it on your books as an expense (or outflow). It is that easy.

Cash Basis accounting has many benefits, including simple and straightforward reporting. Cash Flow is explicitly stated. Well-suited for small businesses and those owning fewer properties with less tenants. However, there are restrictions to using cash basis for your tax return; states and the federal government can differ on these as well, and there can be restrictions on choosing Accrual Basis and then switching to Cash Basis accounting, and vice versa. Another reason it is imperative to get input from your professional team when choosing an accounting basis.

The most common issue with Cash Basis accounting is the reporting, more specifically the inconsistency of reporting over short periods of time. The main point to takeaway here is that if you look at your financial statements on a month-to-month basis, the consistency will not always be there. That is because tenants pay late or early, some vendors do not bill and thus you do not pay consistently, so that means comparing one month to another month may look very different. As such, when using Cash Basis accounting, it is best to compare quarter-to-quarter, or even better, year-to-year, and manually adjust payments received and made in December or January to get an apples-to-apples comparison.

CHAPTER 31

Accrual Basis Accounting

Accrual Basis Accounting has almost no regard for the transfer of cash for accounting and reporting purposes, which seems illogical, doesn't it? That is because accrual accounting records transactions when they *should* occur, not necessarily when they *do* occur.

Income is booked at the time a service is performed. So, if a tenant is occupying an apartment, you record the income on the 1st of the month, when the tenant is charged, and not when the payment is received. Let's look at a couple examples.

Example 31.1:

Your tenant pays you $1,000 on the 30th of January for February Rent. This rental income will be recorded on your February Financial Statements, not your January ones (as is the case when using Cash Basis accounting).

Example 31.2:

Another one of your tenant's monthly rent is $1,500. They decide to pay you three months in advance for the first quarter, $4,500, on January 3rd. You would record the rent for each month paid in the proper month; so, your Profit and Loss Statement would show $1,500 income for January, $1,500 for February, and $1,500 for March.

Expenses are counted when the service is performed, or the goods are received. So, if you prepay for January, February & March landscaping, you count one-third of the expense in January, one-third in February and one-third in March. On the other hand, if a landscaper mows your property's lawn, but doesn't send a bill for three months, the expense is still counted in the months that the work was done. The date that you receive or pay the bill is irrelevant. Let's look at a couple examples.

Example 31.3:

You paid a landscaping service $900 for the first quarter of the year in advance, on January 2nd. On your financial statements, you will show an expense in January for $300, in February for $300, and in March for $300.

Example 31.4:

Your landscaping contract is for one year at $300 per month. You pay quarterly, $900, every three months, but you pay at the end of the quarter, not the beginning. While in the above example you paid in January for the first quarter, in this example you pay on March 30th. You will still show an expense in January for $300, in February for $300, and in March for $300. The date that you pay the bill is irrelevant to booking the monthly expense.

Benefits of Accrual Basis accounting include clearer and more correct reporting, so that a property manager and owner can see what occurred in the period in question, and thus be able to better know what income and expenses to expect in the future. Accrual basis accounting is better utilized for large scale ownership and management. It is also much more effective when budgeting and forecasting. Hindrances include not knowing if actual cash came in or expected cash was collected. In a large-scale operation with more money on hand this is not as big of an issue, but for a single property owner, this may not work as well, as we will see in the next chapter.

CHAPTER 32

Cash or Accrual Accounting: Which is Right for You

To decide which Basis will be best for your property or company, it is important to review how the financial statements will look. Let us look at comparative Income Statements (another name for the Profit and Loss Statement) for Cash Basis and Accrual Basis Accounting.

Example 32.1:

Tenant #1 pays $1,000 a month, and they usually pay on the last day of the prior month for the current month. This tenant paid January's rent the previous December, and paid two months' worth of rent, or $2,000 in February.

Tenant #2 has a monthly rental amount of $1,500. They decide to pay you three months in advance for the first quarter, $4,500, on January 3rd.

The first quarter gas utility bill of $300 is paid in February, which covers the whole first quarter.

You paid a landscaping service $900 for the first quarter of the year in advance, on January 2nd.

Here are the Income Statements (aka Profit and Loss Statement) for the first quarter; the one on the left is prepared using Cash Basis, the right one is prepared using Accrual Basis.

Income Statement (Cash Basis) January - March 20XX					Income Statement (Accrual Basis) January - March 20XX				
	Janaury	February	March	Q1		Janaury	February	March	Q1
Rental Income					Rental Income				
Tenant #1	1,000	2,000		3,000	Tenant #1	1,000	1,000	1,000	3,000
Tenant #2	4,500			4,500	Tenant #2	1,500	1,500	1,500	4,500
Total Income	5,500	2,000	0	7,500	Total Income	2,500	2,500	2,500	7,500
Expenses					Expenses				
Gas Utility		300		300	Gas Utility	100	100	100	300
Landscaping	900			900	Landscaping	300	300	300	900
Total Expenses	900	300	0	1,200		400	400	400	1,200
Net Income	4,600	1,700	0	6,300		2,100	2,100	2,100	6,300

Of course, this is a simplified Income Statement and as such does not include every and all the income and expenses that can occur when managing or owning properties, but for explanation purposes this Income Statement suits our needs well. Note that there are other accounts that are used when doing Accrual Basis accounting, and that can get confusing to those without an accounting background or strong knowledge base of accrual basis accounting.

As you can see, month-by-month, the differences between the three months are stark using Cash Basis when compared to the consistency of the Accrual. However, when we look at the quarterly totals, they are the same. That is why, when using Cash Basis accounting, the longer the period of the Income Statement, the more helpful it will be. When using Accrual Basis accounting, this issue will not occur, but it may and often does require more time and more knowledge about accounting practices. Specifically, and especially understanding prepaid expenses, accounts payable, and accounts receivable, which will be detailed in the next chapter.

Most beginning or smaller property owners and property management companies use Cash Basis Accounting. This is primarily due to the fact that it is simpler, and, more importantly, tenants will not always pay on time. Some tenants even go so far as to get months behind in their payments. So, while Accrual Basis accounting means that you have to book the rent the tenant was *supposed* to pay, Cash Basis only makes you declare the income once it has been deposited into your bank. This will lower your taxable revenue because you are only reporting the actual cash has been received.

That is the main reason why, for property management and ownership, especially when starting out, I suggest Cash Basis accounting. As your company and number of properties grows, it may be beneficial to switch to Accrual, but, once you change with the IRS, you cannot go back (as of this writing). Most importantly, any decision to change your accounting basis if unique to your specific situation should be discussed with your financial team. Lastly, remember to choose which accounting basis you will use before you start accounting.

CHAPTER 33

Accounts Payable, Accounts Receivable and Bad Debt

These account topics relate to Accrual Basis Accounting. If Cash Basis is the choice of your company, you will not need to utilize any of these accounts. You can, but it is not required. First off, let us look at Accounts Payable and Accounts Receivable. It is best to think of Accounts Payable (and Accounts Receivable) as holding accounts for cash to be paid (or received).

Accounts Payable is a liability account for bills that have been received and entered into the general ledger but have not yet been paid. Many bills are not due immediately upon receipt. In some cases, terms are even offered for paying promptly, or late fees are incurred, for paying after the bill is due.

For accounting purposes, there are two entries involved, that are entered into the General Journal. The first records the bill being received, and the second for when the bill is paid. Three accounts are involved: an Expense account, the Accounts Payable Account, and the Cash/Bank Account. Let us look at an example.

Example 33.1:

You called an electrician to check on a flood light that was out at one of your commercial centers. He went out to repair it and sent you a bill for $150. Here are the two journal entries needed to record the transaction. First, when the bill is received:

Debit: Electrical Repairs Expense $150
Credit: Accounts Payable $150

Then, when the bill is paid:

Debit: Accounts Payable $150
Credit: Cash/Bank $150

As you can see, the Accounts Payable Account is credited $150 when the bill is received, and is debited $150 when the bill is paid, thus taking the account balance to zero.

Accounts Receivable is an asset account used for rent collection, that has been billed to the tenants, but has not yet been received. Three accounts are involved: an Income account, the Accounts Receivable Account, and the Cash/Bank Account. Rent is usually due on the first of the month, so let us look at the accrual basis transactions to record the invoice due.

Example 33.2:

On the first of the month, your tenant has rent due in the amount of $1,000. On the first, you record the following journal entry:

Debit: Accounts Receivable $1,000
Credit: Rental Income $1,000

The tenant pays the rent on the second. Here is the second entry needed to record the deposit of their payment:

Debit: Cash/Bank $1,000
Credit: Accounts Receivable $1,000

As you can see, the Accounts Receivable Account is debited $1,000 when the invoice is entered and is credited $1,000 when the money is received from the tenant, thus taking the account balance to zero.

To reiterate, accounts payable and accounts receivable can be thought of as holding accounts. Meaning that their balance should normally be zero, but as some bills are not paid right away, and some tenants pay late, they often maintain a balance. The goal is at the end of any period of reporting, their balance should be zero. As you can see in the examples, once the transactions were completed, the balances in each account were zero.

You will often see and hear about employment opportunities for Accounts Payable or Receivable specialists, so it is a very prevalent part of accounting in general. Many businesses use accrual basis accounting, and it can become more difficult depending on the field or business. However, specifically for Real Estate and Property Management accounting, the use of either account as a part of Accrual Basis Accounting is not difficult but does take getting used to.

Bad Debt is an expense account that is utilized by those property management companies and owners that are using Accrual Basis accounting, to reconcile their income accounts to only pay taxes on the actual income received. In Cash Basis Accounting, as income is recorded as it is received, there is no need to reconcile the Rental Income and Accounts Receivable, which are the two accounts used.

As mentioned earlier, sometimes tenants get behind on rent, and sometimes it goes on for a long time, and other times tenants move out in the middle of the night and all you are left with is a dirty rental space and, hopefully, a security deposit to use to fix it up. I have seen both more often than I care to admit, so as an aside, it is always important to check in with tenants, stopping by their rental space or talking with them over the phone, that get behind on their rent, because it can go downhill quickly.

The money you have reported on your Accrual Basis Profit and Loss Statement, meaning the rental revenue you earned, remains in your Accounts Receivable account until you have received the cash payment from the tenant. So, when the tenant has not paid you in a while, or has moved out without paying, you will have an amount in Accounts Receivable that needs to be removed, and it can be removed via an expense account entitled Bad Debt. Let's look at an example.

Example 33.3:

A tenant that was paying $1,000 became delinquent for five months, and then moved out. You had already booked $5,000 but never received any cash from the tenant, so there was a $5,000 balance in your Accounts Receivable. You need to remove the rent that accrued, and the journal entry entered into the General Ledger would be:

Debit: Bad Debt Expense $5,000
Credit: Accounts Receivable $5,000

You may be asking, well, why can't I just reduce the income I received, right? That way it looks like my income is less because it was less since I did not receive the income. No one is saying you cannot do this, but it goes against best accounting practices, and I would not advise it. However, at the end of the day, your net income is still the same.

Some tenants will make a deal to pay partial rent, and the owner may look at the situation, realize they are not collecting anything, and something is better than nothing, and accept that. I worked for one property management company that managed a property that was only 20% occupied. One of the tenants in the building was behind on their rent, but was paying some of the rent every month, and ownership determined that it was better to keep them in the rental space, to show higher occupancy and thus bring new tenants into the center. Many businesses do not want to rent where occupancy is low, so in their case it was worth it to the owner to accept some, but not all of the rent, to get more tenants into the building.

At the end of a period, usually a year, many property management companies and owners will review their Accounts Receivable and determine how much is actually collectable, which helps them determine the amount to expense to Bad Debt. Then, at the end of the period, the company would use the Bad Debt Expense account to reconcile what the tenant had actually paid to what they were supposed to pay. You can determine the Bad Debt expense at the end of the year utilizing a report called Aging Accounts Receivable, or A/R Aging for short. This report is separated by periods of time typically broken down as: 0-30 days, 31-60 days, 61-90 days, and 91-beyond, but it could be for any period. Let's look at an example.

Example 33.4:

Company XYZ owns a commercial center with multiple tenants, however there are three tenants that are behind on their rent. Tenant One owes for the current month, $500. Tenant Two has paid for the current month, but underpaid two months ago, and still owes $300 from that month. Tenant three was unable to pay their rent in full four months ago, $1,500, but has paid every month since. Here is how the report would look, accounting for these three items:

Company XYZ
Accounts Receivable Aging Report
As of December 31, 20XX

Tenants	1-30 Days	31-60 Days	61-90 Days	91 Plus
	$500	$0	$300	$1,500

Many companies have a policy on how they account for Bad Debt. Some will make an adjustment at the end of the year, some will adjust it for all debt over 90 days old, some will only do it when a tenant moves out and/or declares bankruptcy. Just remember, regardless of the method chosen, being consistent is key. Let us look at another example.

Example 33.5:

Company XYZ will remove all bad debt over 91 days at the end of the year from its books. Here is the journal entry, using the Accounts Receivable Aging Report from Example 33.4:

Debit: Bad Debt Expense $1,500
Credit: Accounts Receivable $1,500

A point of note is you can decide how you will apply rent payments. I worked for one management company that operated like the example above, and always applied the rent paid in the month it was received, and then applied it to back-owed rent. Another way to do this, which I saw multiple firms utilize over the years, is to apply payments to the oldest outstanding invoice. Let us look at a final example.

Example 33.6:

Tenant One owes for the current month, $500. Tenant Two has paid for the current month, but underpaid two months ago, and still owes $300 from that month. Tenant Three was unable to pay their rent in full four months ago, $1,500, but has paid every month since. If the property owner is applying outstanding payments made by the tenants to the oldest invoice, their Accounts Receivable Aging Report would only have an amount in the 1-30 days old debt column for $2,300, because all the tenants have made payments in subsequent months from when their delinquency was incurred.

It is very important to note here that when a Bad Debt policy is determined, it is confirmed with your CPA/Tax Preparer, as there may be tax implications in utilizing Bad Debt Expense or reducing Income.

CHAPTER 34

Fixed Assets: To Capitalize or Not to Capitalize

Fixed assets are those tangible assets that cannot (usually) be converted easily to cash, for example buildings, vehicles, land, or equipment, among others. The reason I mentioned usually is that, you could say, "I can take my company's vehicle down to the local used car dealership and sell it today for cash." While that is true, there is also a dollar limitation on what can be classified as an expense and a fixed asset, and the cost of a vehicle will almost always be above that threshold, and thus is a fixed asset and depreciated.

These tangible, fixed assets are found on the business' Balance Sheet. When you purchase a property, you will enter an amount for the property as an asset on your balance sheet. If you buy a company car, that car will be an asset on your balance sheet. These will be offset by either a loan (which will be a liability on your Balance Sheet) or Equity. We will see how the land and building assets are recorded on your books in the chapter titled "How to Record a Purchase Closing Statement."

Depreciation is the term used for expensing part of the value of the fixed asset over time, and we will talk more about Depreciation in a later chapter. For property owners, you will have the building and the land as fixed assets on your balance sheet. For property management companies, you will track the owner's building and land, and, separately for the company, any vehicles or equipment that are used by the company. There are also intangible assets that are found on a company's or owner's balance sheet, such as loan fees and leasing commissions, and these are amortized over time; Amortization will also be discussed in a later chapter.

Capitalized Expenses are those purchases that are used to buy, maintain or improve fixed assets. Many companies will use the IRS limitations to determine whether to capitalize an expense (As of this writing, the current IRS threshold is any expense above $2,500, but this must be declared to the IRS; and is another item to review with your CPA before filing your taxes).

For most owners and property managers, maintenance expenses are usually the most difficult to decide whether to capitalize or not. When capitalizing expenses, you are converting them to assets, which appear on your balance sheet (while expenses appear on the Profit and Loss Statement). Capitalizing expenses can be dealt with in different ways by you and your CPA, and there may be different goals on whether to capitalize or not capitalize an expense, and you will always want to make sure your CPA explains all the options to you, for the greatest tax benefit. This is another reason why it is quite important to choose a CPA that understands property ownership and management.

Monthly landscaping maintains the property, but does not increase the value, and is never capitalized though large landscaping projects out of the normal course of business could very well be capitalized. Usually maintenance done at specific intervals (monthly landscaping, day porter, cleaning services, parking lot sweeping, etc.) is not capitalized. Annual expenses can be capitalized, such as performing a slurry coat on the parking lot or painting the entire building. However, oftentimes they are not, as they are done on a consistent, often annual, basis.

With that being said, the general rule of thumb is: if the Expense is for the long-term benefit of the property (more than one year), by either maintaining or increasing its value, then the Expense should be capitalized. So how does this work? Let's look at some examples.

Example 34.1:

Before a tenant moves into their rental space, they have negotiated to have a new HVAC unit installed at the owner's expense for a cost of $7,000. This expense would be capitalized, as it improves the building asset. The cost is above the normal expense threshold and the unit will be in use for many years.

Example 34.2:

You receive a bill from your landscaper for $10,000. He planted four new trees for a cost of $3,000 and built seven planter boxes on the property for a total of $5,000. Then he did his monthly work for $2,000. As the new trees and planters will increase the value of the property, $8,000 will be capitalized. The $2,000 expense is for monthly maintenance and is not capitalized.

Example 34.3:

Your commercial strip center needs a new coat of paint for the entire building. The expense is $15,000. Your CPA says to capitalize. You say, it's normal maintenance and does not increase the value of the property. This one is tricky, as it could be argued either way, and really depends on the frequency of painting. If it is painted annually, it would be best to expense. If every few years, than it is possible to capitalize. Whatever choice you make, remember that it is you who signs your tax return, not the CPA, and thus are liable for any errors, real or perceived, determined by the IRS when they review and accept your tax return.

To reiterate what was mentioned above, as it is very important to know that when talking to your CPA about Capitalization, make sure they understand where you are coming from regarding capitalized expenses. The best way to do this is to have a company policy in regard to capitalization. Some companies choose a dollar amount threshold, for example $2,500, meaning that any single expense under $2,500 will be expensed, regardless of if it improved or maintained the asset. Others will only capitalize certain items. At one company I worked for they would not capitalize anything, and their CPA would decide what to capitalize.

Always ask your CPA if they capitalized any items on your company's tax return. Review these in detail, because you very well may not agree, as many CPAs will try to show their value to you as a client by capitalizing some expenses when you do not want them to.

CHAPTER 35

Tenant Improvements, Buildouts, and Whiteboxing

These three items are linked to major renovations of a rental space or building and can occur before the tenant can move in, after they move in, or after they move out. In most cases these expenses are capitalized.

A **Tenant Improvement Allowance** (or TI, for short) is a sum of money the landlord provides to the tenant to improve the rental space. This is determined during the lease negotiations between the owner and tenant. Some tenants do not have the start-up money needed to improve or customize the rental to their business, so the owner will provide funds for the tenant to use to improve their rental space to open for business. Usually this will require the tenant to pay a higher rent in later years of the lease, for the landlord to recover his initial tenant improvement investment. An owner is not (usually) privy to what the tenant spends their Tenant Improvement Allowance on, so will capitalize the total money provided to the tenant in TI. Let us look at an example.

Example 35.1:

The owner and tenant negotiate a lease for four years, in which the owner will provide the tenant with $24,000 to improve the space to suit the tenant's business. The tenant agrees to pay back the owner $500 per month for the 48 months of the lease. On the owner's Balance Sheet, they will have a Buildings Improvement Fixed Asset Account, and that account will be debited (increased) $24,000. Here is the journal entry to record the transaction.

Debit: Building Improvement Asset $24,000
Credit: Cash/Bank $24,000

Tenant Improvements are not the same as **Tenant Buildouts**. A buildout, also determined during the lease negotiations, is when the owner manages the improvement of the tenant's space in order for them to open for business. The difference is that the owner agrees to perform all the work, and as such is required to hire and pay all the vendors. Owners will usually choose this route when they have a good vendor team in place, as they will most likely be able to complete the work at a lower price point than providing the tenant with a Tenant Improvement allowance. This also allows the owner to know the exact changes being made inside the rental space. Here's another example to look at.

Example 35.2:

The owner meets a prospective tenant that wants to open a restaurant. The tenant will need new countertops, two additional bathrooms, a hood for exhaust, and a larger HVAC unit. The owner has a dedicated team to do this work, and thinks they can do the work for only $20,000, when the tenant quoted them that the amount they will need is $24,000. The owner and the tenant negotiate a lease for four years, in which the owner will provide the tenant with what they have requested, and the tenant agrees to pay back the owner $500 per month for the 48 months of the lease.

The owner was able to save $4,000, and on the owner's Balance Sheet, they will have a Buildings Improvement Fixed Asset Account, and that account will be debited $20,000. Here is the Journal Entry to record the transaction.

Debit: Building Improvement Asset $20,000
Credit: Cash/Bank $20,000

Whiteboxing occurs after a tenant leaves a space and the owner wants to restore the space to its "original condition." Not the exact original condition of course, but the rental space is completely cleaned, painted a neutral color (often white, hence "whiteboxing"), so a future tenant can decorate any way they choose. Sometimes tenants leave a space in particularly bad shape, or the ownership thinks it will not be rented if the space does not look better. Many tenants are drawn to a clean, fresh-looking space and often pay a premium for that, which is the idea behind Whiteboxing a rental unit. Let's look at an example.

Example 35.3:

A tenant moved out of a space and to restore it to its original condition costs the owner a total of $15,000. On the owner's Balance Sheet, they will have a Buildings Improvement Fixed Asset Account, and that account will be debited $15,000. Here is the Journal Entry to record the transaction.

Debit: Building Improvement Asset $15,000
Credit: Cash/Bank $15,000

Not all owners will whitebox a space after a tenant moves out, and there can be multiple reasons for this. Ownership may not have the funds to pay for restoring the space and would rather wait and see if a new tenant will take the space "as-is," meaning no additional outlay from the owner to improve the space in order to sign the tenant to a lease.

Another possible reason is that a new tenant will negotiate a Tenant Improvement Allowance or a Buildout as part of their lease, and that allows either the tenant or the owner to improve the old space and thus the owner can avoid the direct expense of fixing up the space, by being reimbursed throughout the lease term.

Also, sometimes a space is fitted for a certain type of business (for example, a restaurant) and to change the space for a different business would be cost adverse, and it would be more financially beneficial to seek out another restaurant tenant, which is something I saw often.

Whatever your reasons for choosing to Whitebox, Buildout or provide a Tenant Improvement Allowance, always compare and contrast the best option for your property.

CHAPTER 36

Depreciation and Amortization for Accounting

Depreciation and Amortization are the expensing of intangible and tangible assets, respectively, over time. The time period is determined by many mitigating factors, not limited to, the nature of the asset, the useful life of the asset, the tax implications of the asset, among many others. Your CPA should determine the best way to utilize depreciation and amortization to provide you the greatest tax benefit.

Depreciation and Amortization are non-cash items, so you will never see them on a Cash Flow Statement, and they will never be associated with actual money paid or collected. Many companies do not record depreciation and amortization on their Balance Sheet until the end of the year, simply because they do not want it appearing on their Profit & Loss statements, as it is a non-Cash item. However, as they are expenses, you will see them on your tax return. Many companies choose to show depreciation and amortization below normal income and expenses as an "other expense."

On the Balance Sheet they are also found, and the asset accounts that correspond with Amortization and Depreciation are called Accumulated Depreciation and Amortization. These accounts are considered "contra" asset accounts, meaning they have a normal credit balance (we will see the necessity of tracking accumulated depreciation in the section on Gain/Loss on Building Sale), and offset the Asset Cost they associate with. These accounts are also used to track the amount of depreciation and amortization expensed over the years.

CHAPTER 37

Depreciation and Accumulated Depreciation

Depreciation is the expensing of a tangible, fixed asset over a period of time. Depreciation applies to all fixed assets – **except land**. The buildings on your property can be depreciated as can the vehicles your company owns; if you owned a manufacturing company the equipment used to make your product would be depreciated. There are many different depreciation methods; the most common is called Straight Line Depreciation. Reviewing an example will show us how depreciation works.

We will need three different items to calculate the depreciation for straight line depreciation (other types will need more information, and in those cases utilize your CPA for assistance):

1. The purchase price of the asset
2. The useful life of the asset
3. The cost of the asset when it is sold (residual value)

Number one is easy as you know what you paid based on the receipt. Number two, the useful life, is an estimate of the amount of time (usually in years) that you will use the asset. The IRS has guidelines on the useful life of certain assets, and you can check with their website or with your CPA for that information. The Residual value is the amount received when selling the asset. Well, how would you know that? You just bought it, right? Well, this is an estimation, your best guess as it were. Let us look at an example.

Example 37.1:

You buy a company car for $50,000. The Useful life you estimate at five years, and you go online to see what a five-year-old model of the same vehicle sells for today, which is $10,000. The equation is as follows:

$$\frac{\$50{,}000 - \$10{,}000}{5 \text{ (years)}} = \$8{,}000, \text{ which is the depreciation expense per year for five years}$$

Using the above example, let us look at how Depreciation and Accumulated Depreciation will appear on your financial statements. On your balance sheet you have a vehicle worth $50,000. You will also have accumulated depreciation in the first year of $10,000, assuming you purchased the vehicle on January 1st (Depreciation for the first year and last year of ownership is calculated by the number of days the asset is in your possession). Let us look at how that will look on your financial statements.

Example 37.2:

Here is what that portion of the Balance Sheet will look like:

Fixed Asset - Company Car $50,000
Accumulated Deprecation   -$10,000

The Expense will appear on your Profit and Loss Statement as:

Depreciated Expense $10,000

The journal entry to record the above transaction is as follows:

Debit: Depreciation Expense $10,000
Credit: Accumulated Depreciation $10,000

I cannot stress enough that you should talk to your CPA before you record any depreciation on your own, as they know the IRS treatment for Fixed Assets and will ensure you get the best depreciation model for your assets.

CHAPTER 38

Amortization for Property Management

You will hear the term Amortization often in property management; and let's clear up that these are *different* terms for Accounting and Property Management. *For Property Management and leasing, amortization* means adding a cost to a tenant's monthly invoice to charge them for some cost that you, as the owner, paid at the beginning of the lease (or during a renewal). Let's look at an example.

Example 38.1:
You just leased a space to a brand-new small business. They are just getting started and as such do not have a lot of cash on hand to pay the first three months' rent payments.

They provided you their business model and as they see it revenue will start to be generated by the third month. But the market is hot, and you did not need to offer them rent credits to sign the lease. So, you agree to suspend the first three months' rent payments, and will amortize those three months of rent over the term of the remainder of the lease.

Here is the example in dollars: The monthly lease payment is $1,000. The lease term is three years. The first three months total $3,000. The lease in terms of months is 36, less the first three months. $3,000 / 33 = $90.91 additional is due to you as the property owner per month. So, you will amortize the first three months lease payments over the remaining 33 months of the lease for your tenant.

Amortization for accounting spreads out an expense over time, so while similar to amortizing for your tenants in theory, it is much more like Deprecation. Amortization is the expensing of an intangible, fixed asset over a period of time. Intangible assets include: Leasing Commissions, Loan Fees, Patents, Goodwill (used when selling or buying a company), trademarks, copyrights, customer lists and research & development – among many others. For property management purposes, we will concentrate on leasing commissions and loan fees. **Leasing commissions** are paid to real estate brokers who bring tenants to your property and were discussed in more detail in an earlier chapter. Let's look at an example.

Example 38.2:

A real estate agent brings a tenant to your property, and you agree to pay the leasing agent a commission of $10,000. The length of the lease is 10 years. The leasing commission will be amortized over the terms of the lease, so $10,000 / 10 years = $1,000 amortization expense per year for ten years. So, on your books you will have an Asset called Leasing Commissions for $10,000; you will have an expense each year for $1,000 for the ten years, and your accumulated amortization will increase by $1,000 each year for the ten years. After the first year, here is what that portion of the Balance Sheet will look like:

Leasing Commissions $10,000
Accumulated Amortization -$1,000

Then the Expense will appear on your Profit and Loss Statement:

Amortization Expense $1,000

The journal entry to record the above transaction is as follows:

Debit: Amortization Expense $1,000
Credit: Accumulated Amortization $1,000

Loan Fees are the fees associated with acquiring a loan to purchase a property. The same way Lease Commissions are amortized over the terms of the lease, loan fees are amortized over the term of the loan. Let us look at an example.

Example 38.3:
You agreed to a 20-year loan for which the loan fees were $20,000. There will be an Asset called Loan Fees for $20,000 and then you will have an expense each year for $1,000 for the **twenty (20)** years, and your accumulated amortization will increase by $1,000 each year for the twenty years. After the first year, here is what that portion of the Balance Sheet will look like:

Loan Fees $20,000
Accumulated Amortization   -$1,000

Then the Expense will appear on your Profit and Loss Statement:

Amortization Expense $1,000

The journal entry to record the above transaction is as follows (which will be recorded annually, or until the loan is paid off):

Debit: Amortization Expense $1,000
Credit: Accumulated Amortization $1,000

Both above examples, for Loan Fees and Leasing Commissions, assumed you paid them on January 1st; Amortization, like Depreciation, calculates the first year and last year of ownership depending on the number of days the asset is in your possession. Possession in this case means the day you took the loan and paid the leasing commission. If you pay off the loan or if the tenant moves out before the end of the lease, the loan fees or leasing commission will be removed from your Balance Sheet and expensed on the Profit and Loss Statement.

CHAPTER 39

How to Record a Purchase Closing Statement

A closing statement is a document received from the title company when a property is purchased (or sold) that details the purchase price, any fees, any loans, any expenses and concludes with an amount owed to the Seller, if any. Note that the Seller also receives a closing statement called the Seller's Closing Statement (which is very similar except the debits and credits are reversed). Let us look at an example of the Buyer's Closing Statement. Each row of importance has a corresponding number that will be explained on the following page.

Example 39.1:

1 **XYZ Title Company, Inc.**
2 **Buyer's Final Settlement Statement**

3 **Escrow #XYZ-000123**
4 **Property Address:**
   10040 Main Street
   Anytown, US 00001

5 **Settlement Date:** 11/1/20XX

	DEBIT	CREDIT
Financial:		
6 Total Consideration	5,000,000	
Deposits/Payments:		
7 Deposit from Account #0124		500,000
7 Deposit from Account #9889		1,000,000
8 New Loan From EFG Bank		3,500,000
9 **Fees from EFG Bank Loan:**		
Loan Fee	60,000	
Recording Fee	1,200	
Escrow Fee	700	
Mailing and Office Fees	100	
10 **Prorations/Adjustments:**		
11 Property Taxes	1,750	
12 Prorated Tenant Rents		41,000
13 Tenant Security Deposits		59,000
14 Commission to Agent	10,000	
15 Legal Fees	7,500	
16 **Title Charges, Escrow and Settlement Charges:**		
17 Title Fee	5,000	
18 Title Service Fee	950	
19 Settlement Fee	1,600	
20 Recording Fee	150	
21 Mailing Fees	50	
22 **Due to Buyer:**	11,000	
23 **TOTAL:**	5,100,000	5,100,000

Explanation of Items found on the closing statement:

1. Name of the Title Company Processing the Purchase
2. This says it is the statement provided to the BUYER. The SELLER also recieves a statement from the Title Company. Note the word "Final." Often times you will recieves an "Estimated" settlement statement. This Estimated statement should not be used for accounting recording purposes.
3. The Escrow # used by the Title Company
4. The address of the property being purchased
5. The date that the property is transferred from the Buyer to the Seller
6. also known as the Sale Price of the Property
7. Cash paid to Title Company by Buyer
8. Loan taken on by Buyer
9. These are all fees the bank charges (and there may be others) when it issues a loan
10. These are adjustments required as the seller may have paid expenses or collected revenue for a future period that the Buyer is entitled to.
11. A pre-payment made by the seller
12. A collection of future revenue by the seller.
13. These are security deposits paid by the tenants to the Seller.
14. These are payments to a professional for assisting in the purchasing of the property
15. These are payments to a professional for assisting in the purchasing of the property
16. These are all fees charged by the Title Company and associated professionals (and there may be others) to process the Sale of the Property
17. This is the remainder after all the above transactions have been recorded. Sometimes it is an amount due to the Seller
18. These are fees associated with closing.
19. These are fees associated with closing.
20. These are fees associated with closing.
21. These are fees associated with closing.
22. This is the amount due to the Buyer; depending on circumstances, it could be Due to the Seller as well.
23. This is the total of all the Debits and Credits in the Sale of the Property.

As you can see, there can be a lot of information on a closing statement, however, for accounting purposes, it is very straightforward to record. The left column is the Debit column, and the right is the Credit column. You can make an adjusting journal entry and record it exactly how it looks on the statement. Here is the Adjusting Journal Entry to record (Example 39.2), along with descriptions and information to describe the nature of the account chosen. Entry #1 is the opening of the bank account and to record the owner's equity. Entry #2 is recording the closing statement.

Example 39.2:

Date of Journal Entry				
10/1/20XX	#1			On 10/1, opened the bank accounts
Bank Account #0124		550,000		Balance in Bank Account on 10/1/20XX
Bank Account #9889		1,050,000		Balance in Bank Account on 10/1/20XX
Owner's Equity			1,600,000	This could also be a Liability Account if a loan was taken out.
11/1/20XX	#2			
Building		4,000,000		The total Consideration is split using the 80/20 Building/Land Rule.
Land		1,000,000		The total Consideration is split using the 80/20 Building/Land Rule.
Bank Account #0124			500,000	Cash paid to Title Company by Buyer
Bank Account #9889			1,000,000	Cash paid to Title Company by Buyer
EFG Bank Loan			3,500,000	Loan Assumed by Buyer
Loan Fees		62,000		Total of Loan Fees from Closing Statement
Property Tax Expense			1,750	A pre-payment of Property Taxes made by the seller
Rental Income			41,000	A collection of future revenue by the seller; These are tenants that pre-pay their rents
Security Deposits			59,000	These are security deposits paid by the tenants to the Seller.
Commissions Expense		10,000		These are payments to a professional for assisting in the purchasing of the property
Legal Expense		7,500		These are payments to a professional for assisting in the purchasing of the property
Title/Escrow/Settlement Expense		7,750		Total of Title/Escrow/Settlement Fees from Closing Statement
Bank Account #0124		11,000		A bank wire was sent from the Seller to the Buyer, increasing the amount in the bank account

Note that the Building and Land are done at an 80/20 split, meaning 80% of the purchase price will be booked to the Building (and thus depreciated) and 20% to Land (which cannot be depreciated). There are other ways to allocate this, however the 80/20 rule is the simplest. Discuss with your accountant and financial team the best option to choose for your property.

You will also see detail for Title Fees, Escrow Fees, Settlement Charges, and other expenses that are part of the closing; on the example these have been combined, as for accounting purposes they can be grouped and usually summarized when recording on a company's accounting books, but the level of detail is up to you. You will need to provide a copy of the closing statement to your CPA when tax preparation time comes, so ensure you keep a copy.

CHAPTER 40

Gain or Loss on Building Sale

At some point you may sell your property. If that never occurs and your property continues to generate revenue and you pass it on to your heirs, that is great. But sometimes properties are sold, and in that case the sale of the property can generate a taxable gain or loss. That gain or loss is not going to be the difference from what you bought it for minus what you sold it for, though that is a very simple way to look at it. For bookkeeping purposes, here is an example.

Example 40.1:

You bought your first property five years ago for $1,000,000; and you sold it for $3,000,000. Your gain appears to be $2,000,000, right? Unfortunately, no, as there are other factors at play here.

First off, in those five years you increased the cost basis of the property by doing improvements. You replaced the roof at a cost of $100,000 and installed a brand-new HVAC system for a cost of $50,000. You also purchased an easement for $150,000 so you could increase the size of the parking lot. So now the total cost basis of your property is $1,300,000 ($1,000,000 + 100,000 + 50,000 + 150,000 = $1,300,000).

Secondly, we need to factor in deprecation. As mentioned above, the accumulated depreciation that has occurred in the five years owning the building must be factored into the Gain/Loss on the sale of your property. This should be calculated by your CPA, and they can provide the accumulated depreciation to you. For our example the accumulated depreciation is $180,000.

By taking the Cost Basis of $1,300,000 and subtracting the accumulated depreciation of $180,000 gives us an Adjusted Basis of $1,120,000. Lastly, selling expenses found on the Closing Statement will also be used to calculate the Gain/Loss. For our example the selling costs are $40,000.

Here is the calculation for your books to determine your gain/loss on the sale. First, we calculate the Adjusted Basis, then calculate the Gain or Loss.

1. Calculate Adjusted Basis:

Cost Basis	$1,300,000
Less: Accumulated Depreciation	-$180,000
Adjusted Basis	$1,120,000

2. Calculate Gain/Loss

Sale Price of Property	$3,000,000
Less: Selling Expenses	-$40,000
Less: Adjusted Basis	-$1,120,000
Gain/Loss on Sale	$1,840,000

Note that this is a very basic way to look at selling an asset and recording it for accounting purposes. To attain the exact cost basis of your property, contact your CPA who should keep a schedule of this and can tell you the amount. Always consult your CPA on recording the sale as there may be other tax factors and consequences that you could be unaware of, and you do not want to be surprised later if your tax owed is higher than expected.

PART V

Sample Company: Broadway Avenue Property

In this final part we are going to create a sample property, called Broadway Avenue Property. In the first section, we will perform a Quarterly cycle, using Cash Basis Accounting, for the First Quarter (January, February, and March). We will utilize the following items to illustrate the accounting behind the transactions and thus the financial statements: Journal Entries, Invoicing, Chart of Accounts, Financial Statements, Closing Statement and Rent Rolls; utilizing and incorporating much of the information you have already read in prior chapters.

CHAPTER 41

Section 1: First Quarter, Year One

A. We will use four-digit Account Numbers and here is the **Chart of Accounts** we will utilize to record the accounting transactions:

1000	Cash/Bank Account
1400	Building
1500	Land
1600	Loan Fees
1700	Leasing Commissions
2000	Loan
2200	Security Deposits
3000	Equity
4000	Rental Income
4100	Late Fee Income
6000	Landscaping

6100	Trash
6200	Electric
6300	Water
6400	HVAC
6500	Property Taxes Paid
6600	Insurance
6700	Repairs and Maintenance
7000	Legal Fees
7100	Settlement Fees
7200	Interest Expense

B. On January 1st, you purchase a Commercial Property on Broadway Avenue with four rental spaces, for one million dollars. Here is the journal entry to record the **Closing Statement**, dated 1/1/XX:

		Debit	Credit
1400	Building	800,000	
1500	Land	200,000	
1000	Cash/Bank Account		533,000
2000	Loan		500,000
1600	Loan Fees	50,000	
6200	Property Taxes Paid	5,000	
4000	Rental Income		10,000
2200	Security Deposits		20,000
6300	Legal Fees	3,000	
6400	Settlement Fees	5,000	
		1,063,000	1,063,000

C. Important Items of Note:

- The $500,000 loan will be repaid $5,000 a month, with $500 of that interest and the rest principal; it will commence immediately, and the first payment is due by the last day of the month.
- $633,000 was deposited into the Bank Account on January 1st by the owner, which is the Equity on the Balance Sheet, of which $523,000 was paid to the seller at closing.
- Tenant #1 pays $10,000 monthly in Rent, tenant #2 pays $3,000, and Tenant #3 pays $7,000 monthly for their rent, respectively. There is also one rental space vacant. Tenant #1 paid their rent in December of the prior year, that is why there is $10,000 of Rental Income on the Closing Statement.

- The Tenants are required to pay Common Area Maintenance, Property Taxes and Insurance, as they have Triple Net Leases. Property Taxes are not due until September. You have received the Insurance bill for the first quarter in the amount of $3,000, and that is due by February 15th. The HVAC Bill is received near the end of the quarter, and that amount is $300.
- Each Tenant has a Security Deposit on file equal to their monthly rent amount for a total of $20,000, respectively.
- Included in Common Area Maintenance, there are five expenses: Landscaping, Trash, Water, HVAC Maintenance and Electric, which is for the building lighting. Landscaping, Trash and Electric are paid monthly. Water and HVAC Maintenance are paid quarterly, and you have received the quarterly bills for Water for $500 and HVAC for $300, but do not have to pay them until February 15th.

D. Tenant Monthly Invoices: For Three (3) Tenants

Barrington Property Management

INVOICE

Property: Broadway Avenue

DATE: January 1st, 2023
INVOICE # 101

Bill To:
Tenant 1
1000 Broadway Avenue Unit 1
Anywhere, USA 99999

DESCRIPTION	AMOUNT
Rent (Broadway Avenue Unit 1)	$8,000
CAM (pro-rata share)	$1,300
Property Taxes (pro-rata share)	$500
Insurance (pro-rata share)	$200
TOTAL	$ 10,000.00

Make all checks payable to Barrington Property Management

THANK YOU FOR YOUR BUSINESS!

Barrington Property Management

Property: Broadway Avenue

DATE:	January 1st, 2023
INVOICE #	102

INVOICE

Bill To:
Tenant 2
1000 Broadway Avenue Unit 2
Anywhere, USA 99999

DESCRIPTION	AMOUNT
Rent (Broadway Avenue Unit 2)	$2,200
CAM (pro-rata share)	$550
Property Taxes (pro-rata share)	$200
Insurance (pro-rata share)	$50
TOTAL	**$ 3,000.00**

Make all checks payable to Barrington Property Management

THANK YOU FOR YOUR BUSINESS!

Barrington Property Management   INVOICE

Property: Broadway Avenue

DATE: January 1st, 2023
INVOICE #: 103

Bill To:
Tenant 3
1000 Broadway Avenue Unit 3
Anywhere, USA 99999

DESCRIPTION	AMOUNT
Rent (Broadway Avenue Unit 3)	$5,500
CAM (pro-rata share)	$950
Property Taxes (pro-rata share)	$400
Insurance (pro-rata share)	$150
TOTAL	$ 7,000.00

Make all checks payable to Barrington Property Management

THANK YOU FOR YOUR BUSINESS!

E. January Transactions:

On January 2nd, you receive the rent from Tenant #2 and Tenant #3. Here is the Journal Entry to record depositing the Rental Income:

1000 Cash/Bank $10,000
4000 Rent $10,000

On January 5th, you receive and pay the following bills: Landscaping for $200, Trash for $300 and Electric for $400. Here are the journal entries to record the payments made:

6000 Landscaping $200
1000 Cash/Bank $200
6100 Trash $300
1000 Cash/Bank $300
6200 Electric $400
1000 Cash/Bank $400

On January 20th, you receive a call from the Tenants that there is a water leak. You call a plumber, and they report to you that there is a pipe that runs into the building that will need to be replaced. The cost is $2,500 and they can complete the work that day. The plumber does the work and sends you a bill. You write them a check on January 23rd. Here is the Journal Entry to record the payment:

6700 Repairs/Maintenance $2,500
1000 Cash Bank $2,500

On January 25th, you pay the Interest on the Loan. Here is the Journal Entry to record the payment:

2000 Loan   *$4,500*
7200 Interest *$ 500*
1000 Cash/Bank   *$5,000*

On January 30th, Tenant #1 pays you their rent, $10,000. Here is the Journal Entry to record the deposit:

1000 Cash/Bank $10,000
4000 Rent   *$10,000*

F. February Transactions:
On February 1st, you receive the rent from Tenant #2 and Tenant #3. Here is the Journal Entry to record depositing the Rental Income:

1000 Cash/Bank $10,000
4000 Rent   *$10,000*

On February 5th, you receive and pay the following bills: Landscaping for $200, Trash for $300, and Electric for $400. Here are the journal entries to record the payments made:

6000 Landscaping   *$200*
1000 Cash/Bank   *$200*
6100 Trash   *$300*
1000 Cash/Bank   *$300*
6200 Electric   *$400*
1000 Cash/Bank   *$400*

On February 10th, you make a payment to the Insurance Company. Here is the journal entry to record the payment made:

6600 Insurance $3,000
1000 Cash/Bank $3,000

On February 14th, you receive a call from your HVAC contractor, and one of the units needs to be repaired, for a cost of $700. They must order a piece of equipment, and that will not arrive until the next week. You agree to the work, and they send you a bill once they have completed the work, that you pay on February 21st. Here is the journal entry to record the payment made:

6400 HVAC $700
1000 Cash/Bank $700

On February 23rd, you sign a lease with a new tenant, Tenant #4, for five years. They occupy the same size space and pay the same rental rate as Tenant #1 and will begin their lease on March 1st. They write you a check when they sign the lease for the first month rent of $10,000 and the Security Deposit in the same amount. Here is the Journal Entry to record the deposit:

1000 Cash/Bank $20,000
2200 Security Deposits $10,000
4000 Rent $10,000

Tenant #4 had a leasing agent, and you have agreed to pay them a leasing commission of 10% of the rent for the first two years of the lease, or $2,000. Here is the entry to record the leasing commission payment:

1700 Leasing Commissions $2,000
1000 Cash/Bank $2,000

On February 25th, you pay the Interest on the Loan. Here is the Journal Entry to record the payment:

```
2000 Loan        $4,500
7200 Interest    $  500
1000 Cash/Bank           $5,000
```

On February 25th, your landscaper calls and tells you that you have two dead trees in the front of your building, and they need to be replaced, and the estimated cost is $1,500. You agree, and they replace the trees the next day. When you receive the bill on the 27th, you notice that the actual amount of the bill was only $1,400. You pay the bill on February 28th. Here is the journal entry to record the payment made:

```
6000 Landscaping  $1,400
1000 Cash/Bank            $1,400
```

G. March Transactions:

On March 2nd, you receive the rent from Tenant #1 and Tenant #2 but not Tenant #3. Here is the Journal Entry to record depositing the Rental Income:

```
1000 Cash/Bank  $10,000
4000 Rent                $10,000
```

On March 3rd, you receive and pay the following bills: Landscaping for $200, Trash for $300, and Electric for $400. Here are the journal entries to record the payments made:

6000 Landscaping	$200
1000 Cash/Bank	$200
6100 Trash	$300
1000 Cash/Bank	$300
6200 Electric	$400
1000 Cash/Bank	$400

On March 5th, you call Tenant #3, as you have still not received their rent. You inform them that there is a 5% late fee for payments received after the 5th per the terms of their lease, and they will need to pay that along with the regular rent of $7,000, for a total of $7,350. They tell you they understand and will pay you next week.

On March 10th, you make a payment to the HVAC Company and the water company. Here is the journal entry to record the payments made:

6400 HVAC	$300
1000 Cash/Bank	$300
6300 Water	$450
1000 Cash/Bank	$450

On March 15th, you receive the payment from Tenant #3 for the full amount of the rent including the late fee: Here is the journal entry to record the deposit:

1000 Cash/Bank	$7,350
4000 Rent	$7,000
4100 Late Fee Income	$ 350

On March 25th, you pay the Interest on the Loan. Here is the Journal Entry to record the payment:

2000 Loan $4,500
7200 Interest $ 500
1000 Cash/Bank $5,000

On March 30th, you receive and deposit the rent from Tenant #1, for $10,000. Here is the journal entry to record the deposit:

1000 Cash/Bank $10,000
4000 Rent $10,000

Let us now look at the financial statements, Balance Sheet and Profit and Loss Statement, for the 1st Quarter. We will Compare the Statements on the Purchase Date, January 1st, and the end of the first quarter, March 31.

H. The **Comparative Balance Sheet**, comparing January 1st to March 31st. Note that the Total Assets = Total Liabilities + Total Equity.

Broadway Ave Property
Balance Sheet
as of March 31, 20X7

		1/1/X7	3/31/X7
1000	Cash/Bank Account	$100,000	$152,300
1400	Building	800,000	800,000
1500	Land	200,000	200,000
1600	Loan Fees	50,000	50,000
1700	Leasing Commissions		2,000
Total Assets		1,150,000	1,204,300
2000	Loan	500,000	486,500
2200	Security Deposits	20,000	30,000
Total Liabilities		520,000	516,500
3000	Equity	633,000	633,000
	Net Income	(3,000)	54,800
Total Equity		630,000	687,800
Total Liabilities + Equity		$1,150,000	$1,204,300

I. The **Profit and Loss Statement** for the First Quarter:

Broadway Ave Property
Profit and Loss Statement
For the Period of January 1 - March 31, 20X7

4000	Rental Income	$80,000
4100	Late Fee Income	350
	Gross Income	80,350
6000	Landscaping	2,000
6100	Trash	900
6200	Electric	1,200
6300	Water	450
6400	HVAC	1,000
6500	Property Taxes Paid	5,000
6600	Insurance	3,000
6700	Repairs and Maintenance	2,500
7000	Legal Fees	3,000
7100	Settlement Fees	5,000
7200	Interest Expense	1,500
	Total Expenses	25,550
	Net Income	$54,800

J. The **Rent Roll** for Year One:

Rent Roll: Broadway Avenue Property
Property Address: 123-129 Broadway
Month/Year: **December 20X7**

Address	Tenant Name	Square Footage	Base Rent	CAM	Taxes	Insurance	Total
123 Broadway	Tenant 1	2000	$ 8,000	$ 1,300	$ 500	$ 200	$ 10,000
125 Broadway	Tenant 2	1000	$ 2,200	$ 550	$ 200	$ 50	$ 3,000
127 Broadway	Tenant 3	1500	$ 5,500	$ 950	$ 400	$ 150	$ 7,000
129 Broadway	Tenant 4	2000	$ 8,000	$ 1,300	$ 500	$ 200	$ 10,000
Total:		6500	$ 23,700	$ 4,100	$ 1,600	$ 600	$ 30,000

Address	Tenant Name	Lease Start	Lease End	Rent Increase Month	Rent Increase Amt	Lease Renewal?
123 Broadway	Tenant 1	5/1/X4	5/1/X9	May	3% of Base Rent	1; 3 year option
125 Broadway	Tenant 2	1/1/X1	M2M	January	$200	None
127 Broadway	Tenant 3	3/1/X4	3/1/X9	March	5% of Base Rent	2; 5 year option
129 Broadway	Tenant 4	3/1/X8	3/1/X9	March	7% of Base Rent	1; 5 year option

CHAPTER 42

Section 2: Two Years Later

It has now been two years, and the Broadway Avenue Property is doing well. We will look at the comparative Balance Sheet and Profit and Loss Statement, as well as the Rent Roll at the end of the second year, which we will need to utilize to perform a two-year Triple Net Reconciliation.

K. Major Items to note:

It was decided that you do not want to track Depreciation or Amortization nor any Taxes besides property taxes on the Financial Statements and allow your CPA to track these for Tax Return purposes. Note that many companies will prepare Financial Statements that utilize EBITDA, or Earnings Before Income Tax, Depreciation, and Amortization (for our purposes in this example, these are not necessary).

During the second year, all the tenants saw their base rent increase, which is detailed on the Rent Roll. There was not enough time to perform a Triple Net Reconciliation; you decided that you would perform one after the second year.

You, as the owner, took draws during year two, meaning you withdrew cash from the bank account and transferred it to your personal account. The accounting implication of this reduces Owner Equity. The draw amount was $150,000 total. Some companies track these separately, and the CPA will need to be made aware of these withdrawals. In this case, the draw will reduce the Equity Account.

L. The **Comparative Profit and Loss Statement**

Broadway Ave Property
Profit and Loss Statement
Comparing the Periods 1/1/X7 to 12/31/X7 and 1/1/X8 to 12/31/X8

		12/31/X7	12/31/X8	Change
4000	Rental Income	210,000	297,070	87,070
4100	Late Fee Income	1,050	1,400	350
	Gross Income	211,050	298,470	87,420
6000	Landscaping	4,400	3,500	(900)
6100	Trash	3,600	3,600	0
6200	Electric	4,800	5,500	700
6300	Water	1,800	2,200	400
6400	HVAC	1,900	3,300	1,400
6500	Property Taxes Paid	22,000	25,000	3,000
6600	Insurance	6,000	7,400	1,400
6700	Repairs and Maintenance	25,000	28,000	3,000
7000	Legal Fees	3,000	0	(3,000)
7100	Settlement Fees	5,000	0	(5,000)
7200	Interest Expense	18,000	18,000	0
	Total Expenses	95,500	96,500	1,000
	Net Income	115,550	201,970	86,420

M. Comparative Profit and Loss Statement Analysis

There is a third column on the Profit and Loss Statement, that is the difference between the two columns (in this case the current and prior year). Most accounting software will provide this column as an option. I highly suggest you utilize it, as it makes it clear what the changes were year-over-year, or period-over-period. You and your accountant or bookkeeper can examine the changes and determine why they have occurred.

Let's start looking at Gross Income. Rental Income is up because the tenants all saw a base rent increase in year two, as well as there was a full year of occupancy for Tenant #4, as opposed to only nine months the prior year. Late Fee Income was slightly up, but that can be seen as worrisome, because it means a tenant, or tenants, were late more times than the prior year.

If we look at the total expenses, we see expenses were only $1,000 higher in the second year than the first. Good, right? Well, yes, but once we look deeper, we notice that in year two there were no settlement or legal fees since those were found on the closing statement when the property was purchased. So, if we remove those, which were $8,000 total in year one, we have $9,000 more in real expenses in year two. Thus, we need to see what these are made up of.

Utilities were up but not greatly, and that can usually be attributable to rising costs and, in this case, the full year of occupancy for Tenant #4 more than likely contributed to that. Property Taxes were higher by a more substantial amount; it may be time to enlist one of those companies that works to lower property taxes. Insurance was also higher, and thus it may be time to get bids from other agents/carriers.

HVAC was higher, and that can be attributable to having to replace a broken air conditioning unit for Tenant #3. You also will want to examine Repairs and Maintenance, for any out of the ordinary expenses; in this case, the Repairs and Maintenance were all in good standing.

Overall, the Net Income was higher by a substantial amount than the prior year, and thus we should be happy to see that. But we always want to inspect and know why Income was higher and Expenses were higher (or lower) to give us the best and fullest picture of how the property is operating.

N. The **Comparative Balance Sheet**

Broadway Ave Property
Balance Sheet
Comparing the Periods Ending 12/31/X7 and 12/31/X8

		12/31/X7	12/31/X8	Change
1000	Cash/Bank Account	166,550	158,520	(8,030)
1400	Building	800,000	800,000	0
1500	Land	200,000	200,000	0
1600	Loan Fees	50,000	50,000	0
1700	Leasing Commissions	2,000	2,000	0
Total Assets		1,218,550	1,210,520	(8,030)
2000	Loan	440,000	380,000	(60,000)
2200	Security Deposits	30,000	30,000	0
Total Liabilities		470,000	410,000	(60,000)
3000 Equity		633,000	598,550	(34,450)
Net Income		115,550	201,970	86,420
		748,550	800,520	51,970
Total Liabilities + Equity		1,218,550	1,210,520	(8,030)

O. Comparative Balance Sheet Analysis

As you can see, the overall changes to the Balance Sheet are minimal, which is normal. On the Asset side of the Balance Sheet, the main changes are to the Cash/Bank Account, which had the following changes from the end of year one, to the end of year two, occur:

Total Income deposited of $298,470; less the owner draw of $150,000; less the loan reduction payments of $60,000; less the expenses paid of $96,500; account for the changes of $8,030. The other accounts, fixed tangible and intangible assets, do not change over time until they are disposed of (sold or expired), except for their accumulated depreciation and accumulated amortization (which we are not booking in this example).

On the Liability and Equity side, the Loan account is reduced by the aforementioned $60,000 in cash payments to the loan service provider. The Equity account is changed by a reduction in the amount of the owner draw of $150,000 as well as adding in the prior year's Net Income (or reducing it due to a loss). The Net Income Amount for the current year is the amount on the current year (12/31/X8) Profit and Loss Statement.

P. The Triple Net Reconciliation

Now we need to perform the Triple Net Reconciliation and send out invoices to the tenants.

First, we need to determine the total amount for each Triple Net Charge, so we can attribute each tenant's pro-rata share to them. The total paid in year one for Property Taxes was: $22,000 and in year two was: $25,000. The total paid in year one for Common Area Maintenance (which includes: Landscaping, Trash, Electric, Water, HVAC, and Repairs and Maintenance) was: $41,500 and in year two was: $46,100. The total paid in year one for Property Insurance was: $6,000 and in year two was: $7,400.

Then, we multiply the occupancy percentage of each tenant by the total amount. For example, Tenant #1 has a rental space that is 2,000 square feet and we divide that by the total property square footage of 6,500 square feet, and determine their percentage is 30.77% (rounded). This is the amount we will multiply each of the Triple Net Expenses by to determine their actual share. The total CAM charges for the two years are $87,600 and if we multiply that by Tenant #1's occupancy percentage we get $26,954 as their share.

The hardest part of Triple Net Reconciliations is doing them for tenants that have not occupied their rental space for a full year. We have one of these here, for the tenant that moved in in March of the first year. So instead of being responsible for the Triple Net Charges for the full two years as the other tenants are, they are only responsible for the time after they moved in, in this case, 22 months, from March of year one plus all of year two.

There are different ways to account for these charges, however the simplest way is to take their pro-rate actual expense amount and multiply it by the number of months they occupied their rental unit and divide that by the total months in the time period. So, in this case, they occupied their unit for 22 out of 24 months so we would divide 22 by 24 to get 91.67% (Rounded), and that is the amount of the annual Triple Net charges Tenant #4 is responsible for. Let us look at the Triple Net Reconciliation Summary and see what each tenant owes or is owed to them.

Broadway Management Group
Triple Net Reconciliation for the Years 20X7 and 20X8

Address	Tenant Name	Square Footage	Collected CAM	Total Collected-CAM	Actual Expense*	Difference
123 Broadway	Tenant 1	2000	$ 1,300	$ 31,200	$ 26,954	$ (4,246)
125 Broadway	Tenant 2	1000	$ 550	$ 13,200	$ 13,477	$ 277
127 Broadway	Tenant 3	1500	$ 950	$ 22,800	$ 20,215	$ (2,585)
129 Broadway	Tenant 4*	2000	$ 1,300	$ 28,600	$ 24,708	$ (3,892)
Total:		6500	$ 4,100	$ 95,800	$ 87,600	$ (10,446)

Address	Tenant Name	Square Footage	Collected Taxes	Total Collected-Taxes	Actual Expense*	Difference
123 Broadway	Tenant 1	2000	$ 500	$ 12,000	$ 14,462	$ 2,462
125 Broadway	Tenant 2	1000	$ 200	$ 4,800	$ 7,231	$ 2,431
127 Broadway	Tenant 3	1500	$ 400	$ 9,600	$ 10,846	$ 1,246
129 Broadway	Tenant 4*	2000	$ 500	$ 11,000	$ 13,256	$ 2,256
Total:		6500	$ 1,600	$ 37,400	$ 47,000	$ 8,395

Address	Tenant Name	Square Footage	Collected Insurance	Total Collected-Insurance	Actual Expense*	Difference
123 Broadway	Tenant 1	2000	$ 200	$ 4,800	$ 4,123	$ (677)
125 Broadway	Tenant 2	1000	$ 50	$ 1,200	$ 2,062	$ 862
127 Broadway	Tenant 3	1500	$ 150	$ 3,600	$ 3,092	$ (508)
129 Broadway	Tenant 4*	2000	$ 200	$ 4,400	$ 3,779	$ (621)
Total:		6500	$ 600	$ 14,000	$ 13,400	$ (944)

Address	Tenant Name	Square Footage	CAM	Taxes	Insurance	Total Owed (owe)
123 Broadway	Tenant 1	2000	$ (4,246)	$ 2,462	$ (677)	$ (2,462)
125 Broadway	Tenant 2	1000	$ 277	$ 2,431	$ 862	$ 3,569
127 Broadway	Tenant 3	1500	$ (2,585)	$ 1,246	$ (508)	$ (1,846)
129 Broadway	Tenant 4*	2000	$ (3,892)	$ 2,256	$ (621)	$ (2,256)
Total:		6500	$ (10,446)	$ 8,395	$ (944)	$ (2,995)

*Adjustment for Tenant 4 - only 10 months occupancy in 20X8

As we can see, three of the four tenants are owed money, due to over collection of CAM and Insurance for all the Tenants except Tenant #2, who was under-collected. All the tenants were being undercharged for Property Taxes. Overall, for the two-year period, Triple Net Expenses were over-collected by $2,995.

As was discussed in the Chapter on Triple Net Reconciliations, it is up to you as the owner on how you want to provide these credits to the tenants, and the leases should dictate. I have worked with owners that would take that amount and put it directly into the center, for example doing an aesthetic improvement with the difference for the benefit of the tenants; I have also seen leases that read over collection by ownership can be kept by the owner if used to further improve the property; or some owners would provide an invoice for the credit and thus the tenant would have to pay less the month the reconciliation was done. I advocate nor advise for any of these, however whatever is chosen by the owner should be recorded in the lease. In any event, if money is owed by the tenant, as in the example with Tenant #2, it is imperative ownership send an invoice and collect this amount, because the owner has already incurred and paid the expense on behalf of the tenant.

Q. Triple Net Changes for the following year

Lastly, we need to update the Rent Roll for the next year with the new Triple Net Amounts that we determined based on the Reconciliation. You have decided to take the Expense amounts from the prior two years and divide them by the number of months of the reconciliation, then add five percent and round up. Here is that Triple Net Changes sheet, using the actual expense total and then adjusted:

Broadway Management Group
Triple Net Changes for Next Year 20X9
Property Address: 123-129 Broadway

Address	Tenant Name	Square Footage	Actual Expense	Monthly	5% Increase + Round Up
Common Area Maintenance					
123 Broadway	Tenant 1	2000	$ 26,954	$ 1,123	$ 1,200
125 Broadway	Tenant 2	1000	$ 13,477	$ 562	$ 600
127 Broadway	Tenant 3	1500	$ 20,215	$ 842	$ 900
129 Broadway	Tenant 4	2000	$ 26,954	$ 1,123	$ 1,200
Total:		6500	$ 87,600	$ 3,650	$ 3,800
Property Taxes					
123 Broadway	Tenant 1	2000	$ 14,462	$ 603	$ 600
125 Broadway	Tenant 2	1000	$ 7,231	$ 301	$ 300
127 Broadway	Tenant 3	1500	$ 10,846	$ 452	$ 500
129 Broadway	Tenant 4	2000	$ 14,462	$ 603	$ 600
Total:		6500	$ 47,000	$ 1,958	$ 2,100
Insurance					
123 Broadway	Tenant 1	2000	$ 4,123	$ 172	$ 200
125 Broadway	Tenant 2	1000	$ 2,062	$ 86	$ 100
127 Broadway	Tenant 3	1500	$ 3,092	$ 129	$ 100
129 Broadway	Tenant 4	2000	$ 4,123	$ 172	$ 200
Total:		6500	$ 13,400	$ 558	$ 600

R. The **Year Three Rent Roll** for January 20X9:

As you can see, the amounts calculated on the Triple Net Changes sheet are inserted here. If we compare to the rent roll from December of the prior year, the amounts have not changed greatly, but are more accurate compared to the actual expense amounts. Also, Tenant #2 had their monthly rent increase. Keeping up-to-date rent rolls and performing Triple-Net Reconciliations, along with reviewing financial statements will all contribute and be key factors in successful property ownership and property management.

S. Notes on **Accrual Basis** Accounting

We have prepared this whole Sample Company using Cash Basis accounting, but we have also talked about Accrual Basis accounting as well in Chapters 29-32. We even compared Profit and Loss Statements between the two to examine the main differences. The reason we will not look at an Accrual example is that Cash Basis can be done by hand, without the need of an Accountant or Accounting software. I would not recommend doing Accrual Basis accounting for property ownership or management without the use of Accounting Software or an experienced accountant.

Any experienced accountant would insist on using Accounting Software, as there are double the number of transactions, since the Accounts Payable and Accounts Receivable are utilized, as we saw in Chapter 33. For simple recording of transactions, or making a simple Profit and Loss statement, a spreadsheet program can be used to prepare using Cash Basis Accounting. This is especially true for one residential property, or just a few.

I have assisted property owners, who only own a couple rental properties, by taking their bank statements and preparing financial statements that their CPAs can use to file their tax returns, but these are on Cash Basis only. If they used Accrual Basis accounting, I would ensure we used an accounting software to ensure correct recording of all expenses and income, including prepaid and past due amounts being recorded correctly. It is up to you to determine how you want to proceed with accounting for your property, and you now have the knowledge and the tools to make an educated and informed decision.

ACKNOWLEDGEMENT

First off, I thank my wonderful wife Jessica for all her support (and proofreading). I must thank my family for their support, always, and a special thank you goes out to my editor (and father), Tom Stribling.

Thank you to all the companies I worked for over the years, this couldn't have been written without the experiences, ups and downs, and getting to know a variety of tenants, vendors, bosses and co-workers, that I've had over my many years in accounting. Thanks also to the teachers I had, so many made such a difference, especially many of the accounting and business teachers I was able to learn from.

This was a labor of love; I really wanted to share all this knowledge that I had accumulated over the years with people who can use it.

Mr. Barrington has decades of experience in the field of accounting, specifically property management, on both the property management and ownership side, as well as the tax side. His most recent employment was for a Private Equity Firm with more than $1 billion in Real Estate Assets, including Residential, Commercial and Industrial properties. Property accounting has always been a part of his life, as growing up he assisted with his family's real estate company, so attained firsthand examples and experience from an early age to know what pitfalls property owners go through. His prior work of fiction, Killer Rabbits, is available where books and ebooks are sold.

Books by this Author

Killer Rabbits, A Novel.

Over. The World. Finished. So fast that the survivors only had two words to describe what had happened: Rabbit Flu. So innocuous a name that no one was scared, concerned, reactionary, until it was too late. Over for most, though not for all.

In one American city the survivors, among them a handsome news anchor, a malcontent alt-girl, a stripper, a gang leader, a transvestite preacher, a millennial disappointment, a reclusive customer service rep, a teenage girl with a penchant for older men, and two soldiers far from home, among others, decide what to do in the immediate aftermath of the near extinction of humanity.

www.ingramcontent.com/pod-product-compliance
Lightning Source LLC
Chambersburg PA
CBHW060503030426
42337CB00015B/1707